# Market Data Explained

# ELSEVIER WORLD CAPITAL MARKETS SERIES

## Series Editor: Herbie Skeete

**The Elsevier World Capital Markets Series** consists of books that cover the developments in the capital markets, as well as basic texts introducing the markets to those working directly or indirectly in the capital markets. Investors are more knowledgeable and demanding than ever before and there is a thirst for information by professional investors and those who sell and provide services to them. Regulators are demanding more transparency and new rules and regulations are being introduced constantly. The impact of competition means that markets are constantly changing and merging, and new instruments are being devised. The Series provides cutting-edge information and discussion about these and other development affecting the capital markets. Technology underpins and is driving innovation in the markets. Inappropriate technology or no technology can bring down even the soundest financial institution. This series therefore also includes books that enable market experts to understand aspects of technology that are driving the markets.

**Series Editor Herbie Skeete** is a well known figure in the financial information industry having spent twenty-six years at Reuters. During his many senior positions with Reuters—most recently as Head of Equities Content and Head of Exchange Strategy—Mr. Skeete has become recognized globally as an expert on exchanges and content issues. He is frequently asked to address conferences and to contribute to roundtable discussion. Mr. Skeete runs the exchange information publisher Mondo Visione Ltd, edits the industry-standard *Handbook of World Stock, Commodity, and Derivatives Exchanges*, which celebrates its fifteenth edition this year, and operates the exchange information website www.exchange-handbook.com.

# Market Data Explained

## A Practical Guide to Global Capital Markets Information

Marc Alvarez

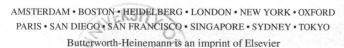

AMSTERDAM • BOSTON • HEIDELBERG • LONDON • NEW YORK • OXFORD
PARIS • SAN DIEGO • SAN FRANCISCO • SINGAPORE • SYDNEY • TOKYO
Butterworth-Heinemann is an imprint of Elsevier

ELSEVIER

Butterworth-Heinemann is an imprint of Elsevier
Linacre House, Jordan Hill, Oxford OX2 8DP, UK
30 Corporate Drive, Suite 400, Burlington, MA 01803, USA

First edition 2007

**British Library Cataloguing in Publication Data**
A catalogue record for this book is available from the British Library

**Library of Congress Cataloguing in Publication Data**
A catalog record for this book is available from the Library of Congress

ISBN–13: 978-0-7506-8055-4
ISBN–10: 0-7506-8055-5

For information on all Butterworth-Heinemann publications
visit our website at http://books.elsevier.com

Printed and bound in Great Britain

07 08 09 10   10 9 8 7 6 5 4 3 2 1

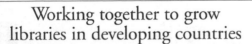

# Contents

# List of figures and tables

**Figures**

**Tables**

# Series Editor's Preface

This book is part of the **Elsevier World Capital Markets Series** which cover developments in the capital markets, as well as basic texts introducing the markets to those working directly or indirectly in the capital markets. Information is fundamental to the capital markets industry. Whether you are a technologist trying to understand market data or a market expert working with a technologist to elicit the best price across market centres, you need to work from common definitions and a common understanding of the building blocks of market data. That is precisely what this book does.

When I was working for one of the world's leading information companies, I would have given anything to get my hands on a book like this.

Marc Alvarez has provided a comprehensive yet accessible survey of the key technical terms used in the market data business. Whether you want to look up a new term that you have just come across, or decode an acronym that has been thrown into a meeting, or find the exact meaning of a carelessly used stock phrase, Alvarez is your knowledgeable and reliable guide.

This book will be invaluable for those steeped in market data, whether as practitioners, technologists, regulators or commentators, as well as for those who are just starting their exploration of this complex yet fascinating area. It will undermine those who use technical terms to obfuscate and confuse, and help to increase efficiency in the industry through improved common understanding.

*Herbie Skeete*
*London*

# Chapter 1

# Introduction

Working with global capital markets data can be a bewildering experience – one of the bigger challenges analysts and other professionals encounter over the course of their career. The volume (about 3.5 to 4 million publicly traded securities by most reliable counts) and complexity of the content (over 500 statistical facts at least) make it seem like a pretty daunting task.

Over the past five years, my work at TAP Solutions has centered on bringing some sense of order to what appears to most people to be chaos. The objective has been to make all capital markets data content available on demand to business users via industry standard, off-the-shelf interfaces. As part of this effort, a significantly large universe of the data content has needed to be categorized and inventoried, with the focus on producing a high-performance relational database system. In turn, this exercise has required the use of a data model, called the Global Capital Markets© data model (GCM for short).

Data models are very useful things. By their very nature, they serve to provide a framework on which data content can be mapped and managed. Indeed, almost all relational database projects employ some form of data model (or they should) as the means by which to lay out the universe of content and how it is stored. The key difference, though, is that the GCM is what is referred to as a *logical data model*. It is designed to serve as a means by which the logic and relationships associated with market data content are communicated to data users. In this way users have a standardized view of market data generated by the international capital markets on a daily basis, and data are made available via standard interfaces to business users.

As a logical model, the GCM is not intended to represent the optimized storage of financial market data. Rather, the model is a coherent view of capital markets data that allows users to interact with the content in a consistent manner, regardless of the source. Essentially, it provides a map, giving a means to navigate through complex content provided by a variety of sources. Properly deployed, such a framework can be used to remove dependence on any data source (such as a vendor or exchange) and serve as a means to integrate the content into a single, conceptually consistent view.

Another application, however, is to provide a general framework for navigating the wide and diverse universe of market data content. This guide is intended for just this purpose – to provide an introductory tour of the logic and general structure that can be applied to capital markets data content. The objective is to provide a conceptual understanding of how the relatively complex world of financial market data is represented within a single framework suitable for business users.

## About data models

The first thing to be aware of is that you don't need to be a technologist to make use of this guide. As mentioned, the goal is to provide a framework for understanding the nature of the content and its associated relationships. It just so happens that a data model provides a very useful starting point, as it already exists and is used in actual business applications.

To keep things as simple as possible, there is very little use of data modeling techniques, and industry jargon is kept to a minimum (hopefully). In fact, only three characteristics from the world of data modeling are used here:

1. *Entities* – probably most easily thought of as tables, entities provide a logical grouping or node within a general framework where items of a similar nature can be grouped

2. *Attributes* – these are the individual items (principally statistical facts as far as the capital markets are concerned) that make up entities

3. *Relationships* – these are the linkages, if any, that exist between entities (and by extension, therefore, attributes).

Taken together and presented as a diagram (an Entity Relationship Diagram), these can be laid out to form a data model. In turn, data models can be used for a variety of other purposes, including building databases, developing applications and even writing books!

For the purposes of this guide, no traditional data model is used. Rather, the key concepts are presented in more familiar forms, focusing on the content produced by the global capital markets and how it can be considered within a single, logical framework.

The result of this approach is to produce a top-down view of this content set. It is a framework that standardizes the manner in which organizations can refer to complex data content, thereby reducing the overheads associated with acquiring, organizing and managing data content.

Using such a framework in turn supports an incremental approach to improving business applications and operating efficiency. It can be applied as and when needed so that new systems take on a standard nomenclature and taxonomy. Ultimately, the benefits of a standardized approach lead to reduced support overheads and faster time-to-market for new applications.

## About data sources

By definition, global financial markets are both complex and very diverse. Considerable effort is expended in capturing relevant information related to the markets. Sources typically employed by financial institutions include:

- Exchanges
- Market data vendors
- Internet websites
- In-house contributions
- Government agencies
- News agencies.

A recurring theme in this guide is the importance of sources for data content. Indeed, the fact that many sources produce much the same content is a key factor in coming to grips with the diversity and complexity.

First, it's important to recognize that most financial firms acquire their market data content from intermediaries. These are well-known vendors, and include readily recognizable names such as Reuters, Bloomberg, Telekurs, Thomson Financial and FT Interactive Data. It is a competitive market – much of the content (stock prices is a good example) comes from the same original source (an exchange in this case). The vendors each acquire, collate and distribute the content as part of their information services.

Second, pretty much by default, each vendor formats and packages the data content differently. There are no (at least not yet) defined industry standards for either format of content sets. Consequently, there is no concordance across all the various sources used by the industry.

Third, it is extremely rare for any one financial firm's data requirements to be met by any one vendor. Indeed, it is not uncommon for firms to subscribe to twenty or more data sources, many of which are duplicated to support global operations.

Taken together, this presents a pretty sophisticated and complex problem for the average data user who simply wants to get his or her hands on the most up-to-date and accurate information possible in order to perform a specific operation. In fact, data sources are so important, as this guide will show, that full attribution of any given value to its source is a fundamental requirement for many applications.

This importance is captured in a fundamental principle that serves as a foundation for the logical framework used throughout this guide:

> *Representation of data content is completely independent of the format provided by the data source, and multiple data sources are supported within the same framework.*

These two points are essential in achieving success when working with market data. One of the common complaints heard in the industry is the lack of consistency in capital markets data across the many vendor agencies. Reconciling these differences is next to impossible without a common frame of reference. Even then, differences in definition, interpretation, format and application persist, making it extremely difficult to perform meaningful comparison across the sources.

## ■ Scope of this guide

The logical framework defined here groups the various types of data content (referred to, creatively enough, as 'data types' throughout this guide). The content is grouped into three main categories, with each category made up, in turn, of one or more subtypes. The three main categories are:

1. *Reference data* – the core of the logical framework, which refers to the relatively small set of identifiers provided by data sources in order to identify particular data content

2. *Business data* – the various sets of content that are used in specific business applications

3. *Static data* – the list of defining values that are associated with specific facts published by data sources. In order to minimize data transfer overheads and space requirements, these values are typically provided as look up or cross-referenced to the actual data by data sources.

The focus within this guide is on the first two categories. Static data, while important, is by definition created as a function of reference and business data. Secondly, static data is by its very nature extremely detailed, varying considerably between data sources. It is therefore treated to only an initial level of detail here.

## Standards and conventions

Much of the content in this guide assumes a basic level of familiarity in working with vendor-supplied market data content. As such, the following conventions have been adopted in order to provide a shorthand notation to aid in understanding the logic underlying the data model:

- Data modeling – very basic 'crow's foot' Entity Relationship Diagrams (ERD) are used, primarily to introduce the basic logic related to linkages between entities. This is not intended to provide a full physical definition ERD, which is available elsewhere in TAP's documentation

- Structure and vocabulary – all the elements discussed in this guide maintain a consistent vocabulary within a structure defined by data types and constituent subtypes. Table 1.1 summarizes the basic structure which is central to understanding the full logical framework.

**Table 1.1**  Data types, subtypes and components

| Data type | Subtypes and components |
| --- | --- |
| Reference data | Primary keys and unique identifiers |
|  | Data source identifiers |
| *Global business data types* |  |
| Security descriptive data | Asset class descriptions |
|  | Conversion terms |
|  | Security ratings |
|  | Security classifications |
|  | (*Continued*) |

**Table 1.1** (*Continued*)

| Data type | Subtypes and components |
|---|---|
| Trading data | Pricing data |
| | Time and sales data ('tick by tick') |
| | Aggregated data |
| | Market rules |
| Ratings | Corporate ratings |
| | Security ratings |
| Issuer & corporate data | Corporate descriptions |
| | Performance data |
| | Industry classifications |
| Relations & constituents | Related securities and membership |
| | Weightings |
| | Related corporates and ownership |
| *Asset-specific business data types* | |
| Corporate actions data | Dividends |
| | Capital changes |
| | Earnings |
| | Shares outstanding |
| | Reorganization notices |
| Terms and conditions data | Summary descriptive data |
| | Redemption information |
| | Floating rate notes |
| | Sinking funds |
| | Municipal bond details |
| | Structured products |
| Payment information | Payment schedules |
| | Amounts |
| | Payment accruals |
| Collective investments | Management information |
| | Holdings |
| | Performance statistics |
| | Risk measures |
| Clearing information | |
| Tax information | |
| Static data | Global lookup data |
| | Asset-specific lookup data |

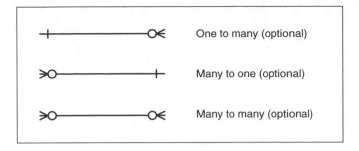

**Figure 1.1**    Relationships used in this text.

Other standards used throughout include:

▪ Entities – only conceptual entities are used. A simple rectangle is used to refer to a conceptual entity or group of entities. Full definition of the entities and attributes is made available within the data dictionary in Chapter 6.

▪ Relationships – these are used sparingly and at a high level to focus on communicating the conceptual understanding. Relationships used include those shown in Figure 1.1. These are the basic relationship types used in data modeling. While there are a number of conventions used in the industry, with varying degrees of precision, these three simple relationships are all that are required in order to construct the framework.

These conventions are adopted here as a means of focusing on the framework rather than any physical implementation. As such, a good degree of license is taken to aggregate relatively complex concepts into more understandable logic. This approach is referred to in data modeling circles as 'denormalization'.

The intention is to take this approach in order to provide a high level of understanding of navigating the complex world of capital markets data content. By focusing on these logical components within a single conceptual framework, market data can be viewed as an independent, single whole. Such a representation is the first step in grappling with the beast, as it provides a common manner in which to refer to specific subject areas, which vary widely, within the full scope of market data.

As part of each section, each entity is therefore defined at a high, conceptual level aimed at identifying clearly its place in the full framework. In turn, detailed definitions of all entities and attributes used within this guide are given in Chapter 6.

# Chapter 2

# Conceptual framework

At the most fundamental level, any data model is simply a collection of related logical entities (commonly thought of as tables) and attributes (fields or columns). In turn, these manifest themselves in various business applications, most commonly databases.

The logical framework here, however, takes this approach to a higher level and has no target applications. Rather, it provides a frame of reference that catalogues and classifies the data content that is used in the industry today. It provides a standard naming convention, using meaningful descriptive English words and phrases, that serves to guide business users through the task of navigating the complex world of data generated on a daily basis by the global financial markets. As a result, it provides a common base upon which professionals can describe and refer to data content, replacing the diversity and variation that exists in today's business world.

Above all, it provides an integrated and extensible framework for navigating the data content produced by the international capital markets on a daily, and in some cases intraday, basis. It presents a pragmatic and readily understood means of working with financial data. In this way it serves the needs of all data business users by providing a single, standard structure.

On the other hand, it's also pretty important to be clear here on what this guide does not intend to provide. It does not imply a front-end application to any one data vendor or other source for financial market content. Rather, it is an independent and consistent description of the global capital markets that serves to consolidate content from multiple sources within a single framework. By design, this open approach is intended to streamline the process for developing and deploying new business applications without needing to account for the substantial and incredibly complex diversity in acquiring the necessary data input from various vendor datafeeds and other sources.

## Basic structure

The framework put forward here is built around two fundamental concepts:

1. Asset classes – high-level classification of financial instruments sharing similar characteristics
2. Data types – information associated with individual financial instruments classified into logical groups or categories. These provide a shorthand manner in which to refer to a series of attributes sharing a common business relevance (also referred to as 'domains').

It is well worthwhile to take a moment to think through these two concepts. The entire logical framework that this guide provides is based on the intersection of these two. They are fundamental to being able to apply this framework in actual business or analytical applications. The following subsections provide a detailed definition of each.

### ASSET CLASSES

A fundamental concept associated with market data is asset classification. In fact, it really doesn't make a whole lot of sense to talk about a particular instrument unless the asset class is also known, at least to a general level. The asset class to which the instrument is assigned, in other words, is a fundamental factor – equities, for example, are traded and processed by firms in a very different manner than bonds, as the two are pretty much separate lines of business.

Unfortunately, the phrase 'asset class' means different things across the industry. Like the term 'reference data', as will be shown later on, the working industry definition is rather imprecise.

The situation is made even more difficult by the fact that there is a wide range of classification schemes in use across the industry with precious little cross-referencing between them. Some of the better-known examples include:

- CFI – the Classification for Financial Instruments from the International Standards Organization
- Vendor schemes – all major data vendors provide various forms of asset classification as part of their services.

At this point in time, various sectors of the industry make use of one or more asset classification systems as required – and for the most part this appears to work relatively well; however, it does limit the extent to which analysis based on one standard can be applied to others. Although the lack of a reliable reconciliation is a major problem, financial firms manage to cope with this diversity by containing the use of asset classifications within specific business functions. Obviously this implies limited re-use of the content, thereby impacting on the extent to which any one data source can be deployed across the firm.

With varying degrees of precision, all asset classification systems provide logical categorization of securities. To meet the objectives of this guide, the question of asset classification can be reduced to a very simple structure, consisting of six main asset classes:

1. *Debt* – financial instruments, such as bonds, that are designed to raise funds through borrowing. Debt instruments typically carry a fixed rate of payment and are secured by collateral. Within this guide, the terms *debt* and *fixed income* are used interchangeably

2. *Equity* – financial instruments that confer ownership rights to the purchaser. These are most commonly thought of as stocks or shares in today's markets

3. *Money market* – short-term (with maturities less than one year is the general rule of thumb) or cash-based instruments. Examples include commercial paper, currencies and treasury bills

4. *Derivatives* – as the name implies, contracts that derive their value based on other, underlying instruments make up this class. Members include options and futures contracts

5. *Indices* – aggregate calculated values that are produced by measuring the prices of multiple securities expressed as a single total value. Indices provide benchmark measures for assessing performance, and also serve as the underlying component for many derivative contracts

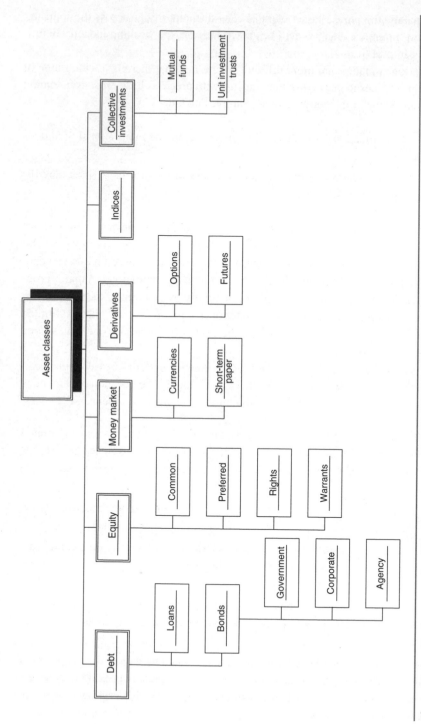

**Figure 2.1** Basic asset classification.

6. *Collective investments* – many of today's most popular financial instruments are collections of other securities. These differ from the derivatives class, as the investor has full ownership interest rather than just an option or right. Examples include mutual funds and unit investment trusts.

Figure 2.1 illustrates the basic structure used here.

This is a pretty major simplification, but these various categories and subcategories prove to be very useful in providing a framework for understanding the business data and how it is applied. A major objective of this guide is to be able to bring any financial instrument into this one, coherent framework. While this high-level simplification is a long ways from perfect, it does provide a layer of abstraction to classify the great majority of instruments traded in today's capital markets. More importantly, it provides the basis upon which to classify other instrument types as needed.

## DATA TYPES

It probably comes as no surprise, but the capital markets produce an astonishingly broad collection of information, reflecting the complex lifecycle of financial instruments, their trading between buyers and sellers and their subsequent downstream processing. Over time, logical groups of this content have emerged and been recognized in practice (if not in documentation) by the industry. However, this process is far from complete – a significant portion of this information remains to be formally catalogued or brought into a single taxonomy. Worse, even where generally-accepted categories do exist, their definitions are not commonly accepted across the industry, leading to a good degree of imprecision.

Therefore, this guide's primary objective is to provide a basic, logical taxonomy that goes across the universe of asset classes and other data content. These categories are referred to as 'data types' throughout this guide.

There are three fundamental data types used in this framework, each of which is made up of one or more data subtypes (which in turn can be made of other subtypes), as follows.

1. *Reference data* – defined as information that describes each corporate organization, the securities it issues and the markets on which the securities are quoted. Within this guide, reference data also refers to data content that is common across all asset classes. Reference data has two main components:
   - identifiers, which are provided by the data sources (typically market data vendors) as the means of identifying a particular instrument, corporate entity or quotation
   - basic descriptive information, such as a security name and its classification.

2. *Business data* – the universe of data types and content that describes or relates to the items identified by the reference data. Data types currently supported within this class include:
   - global business data types, comprising
     - security descriptive data – information that defines specific types of financial instruments issued by corporate organizations
     - market data – information, such as pricing information, related to the exchange or other data source on which a particular corporate organization's specific securities are traded
     - issuer & corporate data – information related to corporate organizations that are identified by the reference data
   - asset-specific business data types, comprising
     - corporate actions – information that describes the events initiated by issuing organizations that affect their publicly listed securities
     - terms & conditions – information related primarily to debt securities that defines the borrowing contract between the issuer and the holder of the security
     - relations/constituents – the universe of constituents making up collective instruments or other items such as indices and corporate ownership structures
     - payment information – details on the cash flow associated with securities and a historical record of when these payments take place
     - clearing information – details related to the post-trade clearing process associated with a given security
     - tax information – specialist content related to the tax treatment likely to be incurred by holders of securities with an associated payment stream
     - collective investments – specialized information related to securities such as investment funds and other pooled instruments.
3. *Static data* – also referred to in the industry as 'domain tables' and 'list of values' (LOVs), amongst other terms. Static data provides a means for cross-referencing numeric and other coded values to a meaningful definition.

From the point of view of the general logical framework, these data types are organized as illustrated by Figure 2.2.

Each of the first-level nodes in Figure 2.2 represents a particular data type. In turn, each data type is made up of one or more subtypes, which in turn can be made up of yet more detailed subtypes. In this way, navigating to the content can follow a drill-down approach, making it easier to focus on just those elements that are required rather than having to deal with the full universe of content provided by any given data source.

For the purposes of this guide, it is also useful to look at this set of content as a series of interrelated entities, as illustrated in Figure 2.3.

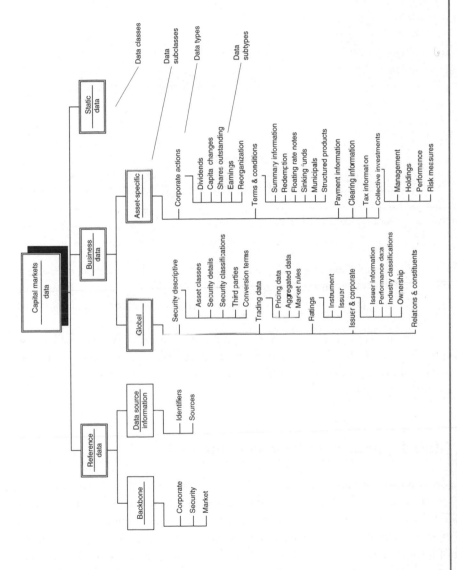

**Figure 2.2** Organization of data types.

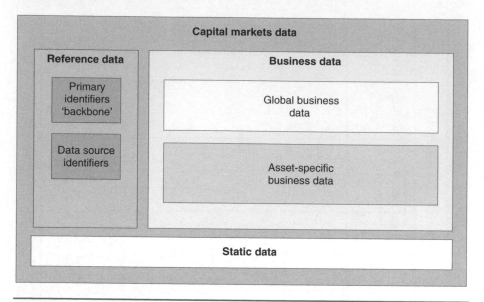

**Figure 2.3**   Data types as entities.

Each of the various classes and subclasses underlying this organizational structure is defined in the following sections. The approach is to 'drill down' within each data type and associated subtypes, so as to provide a quick reference to each component of the data model.

An important point to note here is that the static data class is pervasive, used across the entire framework. While the organization chart represents this as a distinct class within capital markets data, in fact it is closely related to both the reference data and the business data classes.

## Global capital markets data framework

The combination of asset classes and data types provides a useful framework for referring to market data. At a glance, it puts into perspective the diversity of content that is available for a given financial instrument type. Table 2.1 provides this cross-reference.

The cross-reference between asset classes and data types is vital to achieving the goal of a single, coherent framework by which to navigate market data. First, it illustrates clearly that not all data types are relevant to all asset classes. As shown in Figure 2.2, the data classes break down to reference and business data. As shown, the reference data class is pervasive – in order to be considered within the framework, the content must be defined within this class.

**Table 2.1**  Asset classes and data types

| Asset Class | Asset subclass | Reference data | | Global business data | | | | |
|---|---|---|---|---|---|---|---|---|
| | | Backbone | Data source identifiers | Security descriptive data | Trading data | Issuer & corporate | Ratings | Relations |
| Debt/fixed income | Government | ✓ | ✓ | ✓ | ✓ | | ✓ | |
| | Corporate | ✓ | ✓ | ✓ | ✓ | ✓ | ✓ | |
| | Agency | ✓ | ✓ | ✓ | ✓ | ✓ | ✓ | |
| Equity | Common | ✓ | ✓ | ✓ | ✓ | ✓ | ✓ | |
| | Preferred | ✓ | ✓ | ✓ | ✓ | ✓ | ✓ | |
| | Rights | ✓ | ✓ | ✓ | ✓ | ✓ | | |
| | Warrants | ✓ | ✓ | ✓ | ✓ | ✓ | | |
| Money market | Spot currency | ✓ | ✓ | ✓ | ✓ | | | |
| | Forward currency | ✓ | ✓ | ✓ | ✓ | | | |
| | Short-term paper | ✓ | ✓ | ✓ | ✓ | ✓ | ✓ | |
| | Other contract types | ✓ | ✓ | ✓ | ✓ | | | |
| Derivatives | Options | ✓ | ✓ | ✓ | ✓ | | | |
| | Futures | ✓ | ✓ | ✓ | ✓ | | | |
| Collective investments | Mutual funds | ✓ | ✓ | ✓ | ✓ | ✓ | ✓ | ✓ |
| | Unit trusts | ✓ | ✓ | ✓ | ✓ | ✓ | ✓ | ✓ |
| Indices | | ✓ | ✓ | ✓ | ✓ | | | ✓ |

(Continued)

**Table 2.1** (Continued)

| Asset Class | Asset subclass | Asset specific business data | | | | | |
|---|---|---|---|---|---|---|---|
| | | Corporate actions | Terms & conditions | Payment information | Collective investment details | Clearing information | Tax information |
| Debt/fixed income | Government | | ✓ | ✓ | | ✓ | |
| | Corporate | | ✓ | ✓ | | ✓ | |
| | Agency | | ✓ | ✓ | | ✓ | |
| Equity | Common | ✓ | | ✓ | | ✓ | |
| | Preferred | ✓ | | | | ✓ | |
| | Rights | ✓ | | | | | |
| | Warrants | | | | | | |
| Money market | Spot currency | | | | | | |
| | Forward currency | | | | | | |
| | Short-term paper | | | | | | |
| | Other contract types | | | | | | |

Second, static data too is pervasive. Often overlooked as part of datafeed services, this class contains the very details that are required by applications. As such, it too is used across the entire framework and makes use of both proprietary values and schemes as well as, more helpfully, international standards.

This is so fundamental to this guide that it is worth repeating: the relationship between asset classes and data types provides the foundation for the entire framework.

## 'Market' versus 'Reference' data

Easily one of the most confusing issues that comes up in discussions about financial data is the perceived difference between data delivered as a realtime stream (typically referred to as 'market' data) and data delivered on an end-of-day, file-based basis ('reference data'). There is so much overlap in the use of these terms and such a lack of clear definition, this one semantic issue is at the heart of one of the biggest challenges to attempting to bring the universe of content into a single, logical framework.

As far as this guide is concerned, *it is all market data!* Indeed, the only difference between the two is the frequency of update. This guide places no distinction between realtime and reference data whatsoever.

To better understand this concept, it's worth thinking about the data content independently from how it is delivered and used. The reality of the situation is that data content is actually the same, regardless of the delivery vehicle or the frequency of updates.

Perhaps the most easily recognized application for market data is in desktop trading systems (commonly referred to as 'terminals', reflecting the technology heritage of the business). By its very nature, this business function needs to receive data as soon as it is published in order to equip financial professionals with the necessary information (primarily prices) to make buy and sell decisions. Therefore, it makes sense that these systems open up a realtime update stream in order to get these values as quickly as possible – timeliness, obviously, is an advantage in a highly competitive and increasingly automated market.

Realtime pricing, however, is not the only data content delivered to these applications. A significant number of other fields are also provided in order to provide complete context to the pricing stream. This data content typically updates infrequently and on an event-driven basis. Some good examples include:

- New listings – the availability of new instruments in the market for trading (marked by information such as the ticker symbol, security name, face value, currency of trading and so on)
- Dividend announcements – affecting the value of the security depending on whether it trades with dividends attached (cum-dividend) or not (ex-dividend)

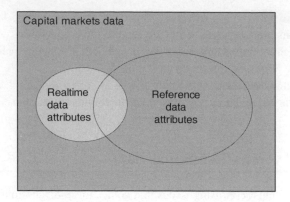

**Figure 2.4** Realtime/reference data overlap.

■ Symbol changes – changes to tickers symbols or other identifiers that will affect how the information is retrieved and made available to the application user.

This content, in case you haven't guessed, is a subset of the 'reference data' universe. And while it updates less frequently, it is important not only to the trading business function, but also in a number of other areas within financial firms, including clearing, settlement, risk management, accounting and so on.

The relationship also works both ways. Realtime pricing is invariably the source used to produce end-of-day pricing records delivered as part of reference data services. These services typically provide far more detail (usually by way of containing many more fields) than is published on realtime services, as they are used for a wide variety of applications within the firm. These are typically referred to as 'back office' or 'post trade' functions. And while different from the trading function (and its associated use of realtime streaming data content, whether within a terminal or any other application), these functions have a broader and deeper data requirement.

If this sounds a little confusing, don't worry – you're in good company. It is a problem that has persisted within the industry for decades and it's unlikely to change any time soon. It's important to note, though, that while there are differences between 'market' and 'reference' data, the applications for the content do overlap, as illustrated by Figure 2.4.

It's important to bear this relationship in mind. However, above all, you should be clear in understanding that it is all part of one universe of content, called here market data.

# Reference data

# Chapter 3

As mentioned in Chapter 2, this guide lays out a framework for navigating the diverse world of data content centered on two primary classes of content:

1. Reference data
2. Business data.

The term 'reference data' takes on a very precise definition within this guide as a subset of the overall universe of market data:

> *Reference data is a collection of facts that describe an issuer, a financial instrument, or a market quote and their associated interrelationships.*

Again, this is a subset of the market data universe, which is categorized here into a series of subclasses.

It is critical to note that reference data has a fundamental function within this framework: it provides the means by which individual items are identified. Secondly, reference data is common across all financial instrument classes. These two characteristics are so important, that this framework treats reference data content as its own class.

## Reference data logic

The division of market data content into the two fundamental *reference data* and *business data* classes is the first step in providing a means of simplifying the complexity inherent to the data produced by financial markets. The first point to recognize is that a dependency exists between business data and reference data. Without consistent reference data to identify the various data items, business data cannot be integrated into a logical whole. It is stand-alone and unlikely to be used for more than one application and, consequently, likely to require additional effort and cost to support.

Understanding the basic logic of the reference data content, therefore, is essential in order to navigate the universe of business data content and apply it to specific business functions.

The basic logic of reference data within this framework is constructed around the following axiom:

> *Corporate organizations issue one or more securities of various types that are quoted on one or more market (such as stock exchanges) by one or more market participants.*

This statement encapsulates the logic underpinning the entire framework. Understanding this concept is essential to applying the model to real-world business applications. Using database representation, this relationship takes the form shown in Figure 3.1.

There is a hierarchical relationship between these key components of the content. As defined below, these three entities – issuer, instrument and market – form the core of the reference data class, and are central to navigating and managing business data content. Collectively, therefore, they are referred to as the 'backbone'.

This framework is fundamental to establishing a coherent view of financial markets. It is important to understand that this 'backbone' is central to all other components of the framework. Indeed, without having the central reference core in place, looking at the financial markets from a coherent, cross-asset perspective is impossible.

By far and away, this central component is the most important logic to understand. It is pervasive in the representation of all data types. The backbone is a fundamental requirement for identifying any and all business data, as it serves the purpose of

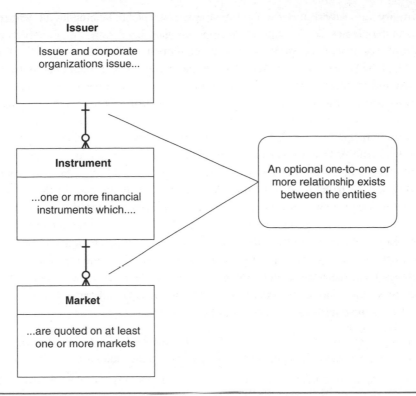

**Figure 3.1**   The GCM conceptual backbone.

identifying uniquely individual issuer, instrument and market-level entities (such as, in order, a company, a security, or a price for an instrument from a specific market).

## REFERENCE DATA COMPONENTS

Reference data within this framework is defined as the set of attributes that perform two very specific functions:

1. They provide unique identification (at the issuer, instrument and market levels)
2. They provide basic descriptive information that fully defines the individual data items identified by the unique identification.

The former is referred to in data circles as 'primary keys'. These are typically alphanumeric or numeric code values that provide a unique identification of the individual record. They manifest themselves as attributes, declared as primary keys, within entities. By duplicating these values between entities, a linkage is created.

Primary keys may sound like a pretty simple concept, but here again it is important to proceed with caution. As with all assumptions associated with capital markets data, the simplicity of the concept masks a complex industry problem.

Indeed, the business requirements for unique identification appear to be so straightforward and intuitive, that it comes as a rather rude shock to discover that no single generally accepted standard is adopted across the industry. Throw in the fact that the requirements for unique identification are essential at all three of the issuer, instrument and market levels, coupled with the hierarchical nature of the relationship between the entities, and the situation rapidly unravels into rather a major mess.

Without any doubt, the single most frustrating aspect of working with capital markets data is dealing with the issue of unique identification. There are many different coding schemes in use at all three levels, with varying degrees of concordance – ranging from none at all to relatively good, depending on the instrument type, market and so on.

Looking at the problem from the point of view of a single cross-asset logical data framework, it's clear that this is a fundamental problem. If unique identification can't be achieved and managed on an ongoing basis, it is likely the framework will fall short of business requirements. In order to support this fundamental capability, the framework breaks the reference data class into two subclasses:

1. *Primary keys* – usefully thought of as a backbone, this subclass contains a universe of identifiers that is independent from any one coding standard

2. *Data source identifiers* – the universe of coding schemes and other forms of identification cross-referenced to the primary keys.

This approach allows for the issuer, instrument and market entities to be identified along with the basic descriptive information in order to provide uniqueness. In turn, with uniqueness defined as a backbone to the framework, the (discouragingly diverse) universe of identifiers in use in the industry at all three levels of the hierarchy can be treated as simple descriptions or cross-references. Figure 3.2 lays out this logical representation.

## FRAMEWORK BACKBONE

The backbone of the data model contains the primary keys and basic related information that serve to identify the issuer, instrument and market entities. The keys used in this framework are:

1. *Issuer identifier* – a value used to uniquely identify issuing organizations, such as companies, governments, and agencies

2. *Instrument identifier* – a value used to uniquely identify financial market instruments

3. *Market identifier* – a value used to uniquely identify content related to individual markets for a given security.

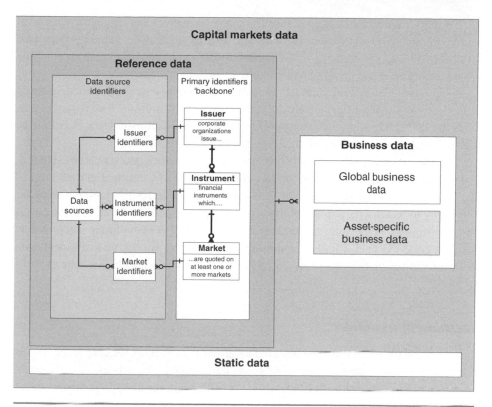

**Figure 3.2**    Reference data subclasses.

In addition, the backbone also contains a number of fundamental attributes that further help to identify data items uniquely within the framework, as shown in Figure 3.2. These entities should be thought of as mandatory wherever possible, as this serves fully to qualify the uniqueness of each record in the entity.

Another key factor to recognize is that the primary keys are independent from any individual data source. They reflect the fundamental characteristics that define uniqueness within the framework, thereby allowing for the diverse world of data source identifiers to be treated as cross-references. This is discussed in the next section.

## DATA IDENTIFIERS

It's probably a good idea to go take a couple of aspirin before working your way through this section. If there's one thing about market data that is going to give you a headache, it is the incredible proliferation of data identifiers that are in use across the industry and around the world.

No matter where the content comes from, and no matter what content at what level of the hierarchy, it is almost certain that some form of an identifier value has been used in order to index the content. These identifiers are made available at all three of the issuer, instrument and market levels.

As pointed out earlier, there is no universal concordance published that cross-references all the identifiers. There are moves afoot in the industry with regard to this, with the ISIN code as a good example of progress at the instrument level, but these are still a long way from becoming the *lingua franca*.

The identifier domain is very broad, and rife with nuance and semantics. The following sections provide an introduction to the universe of identifiers at each level of the hierarchy within the framework. It is very important to recognize the level of the hierarchy to which a particular coding scheme applies – perhaps no other error causes more problems in the industry than applying a coding scheme to an inappropriate level (a good example would be assigning a market-level price to an instrument code without defining the market from which the price was sourced and other related information).

### Instrument identifiers

Likely, the most commonly encountered identifier type is at the security level. This is a direct function of the lifecycle of financial transactions – once booked, the transaction moves through a process of clearing and settlement, resulting in the exchange of instruments. As such, having a clear identification of the instrument that was transacted is a fundamental requirement.

Traditionally, the role of clearing trades between counterparties has been handled by third-party clearing agencies. These agencies can serve as a general industry utility (such as the Depository Clearing Corporation in the United States) or in a competitive market. From the data perspective, though, the most important fact to note is that they all issue their own codes to identify individual instruments.

Since clearing firms operate principally within a given regulatory environment (usually by country), this results in clearing codes being tightly coupled with countries and geographic region. Table 3.1 provides a summary of some of the coding schemes encountered today.

It is important to note that these coding schemes are designed to support clearing and other post-trade operations. A common misuse of these coding schemes is to assign pricing. This obviously doesn't make a whole lot of sense, since in order to create a price the instrument must be traded. Trades take place on one or more markets, as per the original premise put forward earlier. Unless an instrument only trades on one market, therefore, it doesn't make sense to attach a price, since there may be considerable differences between markets – such as the currency, the units, liquidity and

**Table 3.1**    Some coding schemes encountered today

| Code type | Associated geography | Comments |
| --- | --- | --- |
| CUSIP | United States and North America | Widely used internationally; issued and managed by Standard & Poor's on behalf of the American Banker's Association |
| Common | Europe | |
| ISIN | International | |
| Valoren | Switzerland, Europe | Issued and managed by Telekurs SA; both domestic values and international values are issued |
| Wert | Germany, Europe | Official clearing code for Germany |
| SICOVAM | France, Europe | |
| Euroclear | Europe | |
| Various | Australia, Austria, Belgium, Brazil, Denmark, Hong Kong, Italy, Luxembourg, Malaysia, Netherlands, Norway, Spain, Sweden | Independently issued and managed coding schemes issued by official national numbering agencies |

so on. These are all attributes associated, by definition, with market identifiers, as described below.

Another major problem that data users encounter is the lack of a concordance between coding schemes. The International Securities Identification Number (ISIN) goes a fair way to addressing this problem, but does have its own limitations. For example, it is quite common to find that newly issued clearing numbers are not reflected in ISIN numbers on a sufficiently timely basis. As a result, processing tends to continue to be based on the original clearing number independently. Worse, expired and/or deleted identifiers have a tendency to not be purged from databases and other systems.

In addition to instrument identifiers being generated by third-party agencies, they are also generated by data vendors as part of their services. In turn, these are used to a greater or lesser extent by financial firms. Ultimately, this serves further to complicate the issue of unique identification by increasing even more the number of coding schemes available for use.

## Market identifiers

Market identifiers are primarily used for trading purposes. The most commonly encountered symbol type used is the *ticker*. These are usually issued by exchanges for each instrument that is traded. There are also other tickers which are used for trading other instrument types, such as bonds. Some of the most frequently encountered market identifiers include:

- Ticker symbols – alphanumeric symbols issued and managed by exchanges
- QUICK codes – used in Japan
- SEDOL codes – issued by the London Stock Exchange
- RIC – Reuters Instrument Code.

The key factor to understand about market identifiers is that they identify the combination of an instrument and the market where it is traded. As such, there can be (and usually are) multiple market-level identifiers for any one instrument.

This characteristic of market identifiers is very important, as some information that is typically used at the instrument level is actually produced at the market level. For example, a dividend declaration may require different ex-dates since markets have different trading calendars. If an ex-date falls on a non-trading date for one market but not another, it obviously must have a different value. Such nuances can affect both the income produced from purchasing a security and also its liquidity. So while perhaps not a common occurrence, it can and does happen, requiring additional support and expense within financial firms.

Generally speaking, though, market identifiers are relatively simple and intuitive to understand. The one exception is the SEDOL codes issued by the London Stock Exchange. These codes are issued for a variety of purposes, including clearing within the United Kingdom. Increasingly they are being used for cross-border purposes as well, in similar fashion to traditional instrument identifiers.

## Issuer identifiers

Likely, the least structured and reliable set of identifiers used in the financial industry are at the issuer level. Unlike the instrument and market levels, these identifiers are not issued by any industry or regulatory body. While there are a number of issuers in common use, there is considerable diversity in the coverage and method by which they are produced. It therefore comes as no surprise that data vendors have been forced to devise their own identification schemes for corporations and other issuers. Some of the more commonly encountered issuer identifiers include:

- DUNS number – issued by Dunn & Bradstreet, this identifies registered corporations globally and is pretty much the closest to an accepted global standard
- Bloomberg Company identifier

■  CUSIP6 – the first six characters of the CUSIP symbol identify issuers

■  Reuters Organization identifier.

## Reference data in the framework

Since the two reference data subclasses address the need for unique identification, they are absolutely fundamental to using any and all capital markets data. In fact, the reality is that any use of market data implicitly requires the use of reference data (at least as defined within this framework).

It's for this reason that such a precise definition of the term is used in this guide. Simply classifying all non-realtime data as 'reference data' masks this fundamental relationship, leading to difficulties in applying content to business data functions. Indeed, good practice regarding unique identification has a disproportionate impact on applications for business data content.

Another key point to realize, then, is that reference data is a central component to the entire framework, as illustrated in Figure 3.2.

While this layout is an extreme simplification of the complexity of international capital markets, it does serve to introduce several key factors that are fundamental in applying the framework:

1.  Reference data is pervasive. It serves as the backbone to the entire model, acting as the path through which access to the various data types is linked

2.  The individual components can all be used in a stand-alone manner or in conjunction with one another. As long as the structure of the reference data is maintained, any individual component can be used

3.  Each component of the framework covers a variety of associated subtypes. As a result, new information can be added into any classification, or entirely new classes can be added.

Viewed in this way, then, it becomes pretty easy to see how the framework provides a convenient means of navigating to business data content. With reference data defined in this manner, access simply becomes a process of drilling down from the data class-level through the various subclasses, data types, and data subtypes. As a result, any attribute associated with capital markets data is fully classified and presented in a contextually relevant manner.

Perhaps the single biggest benefit to data users of this approach is that it provides a consistent frame of reference for designing applications and carrying out data-intensive business functions. With the content structured and classified in this way, it simplifies greatly the effort required to access data content as part of business applications.

# Business data

# Chapter 4

Where reference data has a very specific definition and scope within the context of this guide, business data refers to a much broader universe of content – the actual statistical facts (or fields) that describe a particular financial instrument. As such, the business data class contains easily the largest number of logical attributes.

As described in Chapter 2, this framework breaks business data into two main subclasses, each of which is, in turn, made up of data types and subtypes. These are:

1. *Global business data* – information that can apply to all asset classes. Constituent data types are:
   - security descriptive data – the information that provides a detailed description of a particular instrument

- trading data – information that captures the details of transactions that exchange instruments between counterparties
- ratings – evaluation of financial instruments and their issuers by recognized ratings agencies
- issuer & corporate information – information that describes the issuer of a particular security. All financial instruments have an issuer of one type or another
- relations & constituents – many securities are made up of other securities (as corporations can be made up of subsidiary firms); it is therefore important to capture all the type of relationship and, if appropriate, the related constituents

2. *Asset-specific business data* – information that is used by the industry by individual asset classes. Data types include:

- corporate actions – announcements and other business events that materially affect the structure and/or value of a security (examples include dividends, capital changes and other event types)
- terms & conditions – these provide details on the legal structure of financial securities (most commonly bonds) and the conditions and schedule under which they may be exercised
- payment information – many securities, and bonds in particular, include guaranteed cash flows to holders made in a wide variety of manners. This information is grouped into this subtype
- collective investment details – related to the funds asset class, this data type captures the information associated with securities such as mutual funds and unit investment trusts
- clearing information – closely related to the trading global data type, this subtype records information to the post-trade processing of transactions, ensuring that buy and sell orders are matched and confirmed (commonly via an independent third party)
- tax information – this subtype records the tax information that is related to the sale of securities; tax information is very important in establishing net values of selling the securities.

Within each of these business data types there can be a variety of subtypes. By working with the data content in logical subsets or modules, the framework is extensible, allowing for the support of both new asset classes as well as data types as new information becomes available. As long as new business data sets are referred to within the context of the reference data described in Chapter 3, they can be supported within this one general framework. In turn, the combination of extensibility and a solid management framework provides a firm basis for identifying and navigating the complex content produced by international capital markets.

In the context of the logical framework, business data can be represented as shown in Figure 4.1.

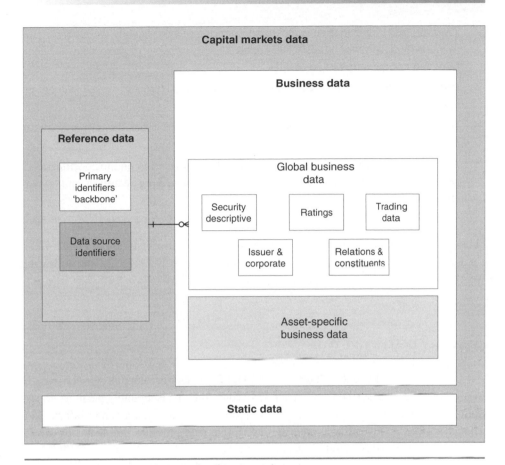

**Figure 4.1**   Business data in the framework.

The following sections provide an introduction to the individual business data types and subtypes. The objective is to present the logic associated within each module and how it relates to the logical structure of the framework. The final level of detail, defining the individual entities and attributes making up each class, is given in the data dictionary in Chapter 6.

## Global business data types

Within the framework, the global business data type is made up of the following subtypes:

1. *Securities descriptive data* – information providing definitions and descriptions about individual securities

2. *Trading data* – information (predominantly pricing) generated by the global capital markets on a daily and intraday basis related to the exchange of financial instruments between counterparties

3. *Ratings* – evaluation of financial instruments and their issuers by recognized ratings agencies

4. *Issuer & corporate information* – information that describes the corporate entity and its business performance

5. *Relations, constituents & weightings* – detailed information on the constituents of securities made up of or related to one or more underlying securities and ownership interests.

These five data types integrate to the logical framework as illustrated in Figure 4.2.

Details related to each of the global data subtypes are given in the following sections.

## SECURITY DESCRIPTIVE DATA

Ultimately, all market data relates to individual financial instruments. As such, next to reference data, as described in Chapter 3, this data subtype is arguably the most important component of the framework. By providing the basic, fundamental information that describes an instrument, security descriptive data provides the means by which content is navigated by asset class and data type.

The security descriptive data type is made of the following subtypes:

1. *Security details* – specific information that defines an instrument

2. *Asset class data* – information, where available, that defines a security uniquely as a member of a specific asset class. The following asset classes are explicitly captured within this framework, as described in Chapter 2:
   - debt
   - equity
   - money market
   - derivatives
   - indices
   - collective investments

3. *Security features* – specific characteristics associated with individual securities

4. *Security classification schemes* – categorization of the security based on various standards used by the financial industry

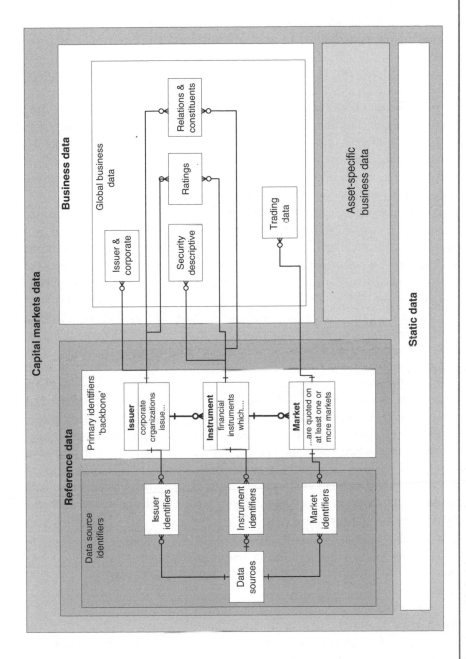

**Figure 4.2** Global business data types.

5. *Third parties* – identification of service provides associated with the security, such as clearing agents, insurers, etc.

6. *Conversion terms* – details regarding the manner in which a security can be exchanged for a security of a different type (e.g. convertible bonds).

Within the logical framework, the security descriptive data type takes the form illustrated in Figure 4.3.

It is worth taking a minute to note the relationship between the instrument entity and these various subtypes. As discussed at length in Chapter 3, securities are identified by an instrument identifier. As such, for any given unique instrument identifier, there is a corresponding link to the various data subtypes that contain a copy of the identifier. Note, however, that this link is optional and not mandatory. As a result, each data subtype only captures information where it is actually used.

This concept highlights an important characteristic of capital markets data: it is entirely possible for an instrument to meet the requirements of reference data without ever producing any corresponding business data. More common, however, is the fact that not all instrument types populate the same universe of attributes. By taking the approach illustrated here, the optional nature allows for business data to be populated only where it exists. When this gets down to the level of a database or application implementation, such flexibility is very useful in avoiding unnecessary complexity and content duplication.

## Asset classes

This series of entities groups the various securities contained in the framework by their respective asset classes. By linking the asset class to the backbone in this way, the framework is fully cross-asset in its support of data content produced by the financial markets. Where there is additional business data related to a particular security, the asset class entity associated to the security type provides a location to capture the relevant content. This can be thought of as a 'gateway' to the business data content that is only relevant to a particular asset class. This content is grouped together later on under the banner of 'asset-specific business data'.

Equally, additional subtypes to each asset class can also be introduced, as shown in Figure 4.1. In this way, not only does the framework extend to support new asset classes as required, it also captures the market data content of specific subtypes within an asset class.

Table 4.1 defines the universe of attributes that are related to each asset class and associated subclass.

Table 4.1 provides a general overview of the asset classes and subclasses typically encountered in today's capital markets. Obviously, this list is dynamic and can be expected to grow in response to addition of new content.

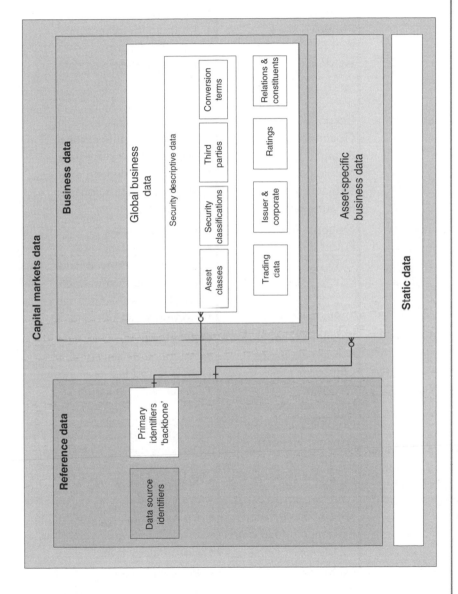

**Figure 4.3** Security descriptive data.

**Table 4.1**  Overview of asset classes, subclasses and attributes

| Asset classes | Asset subclasses | Attributes |
| --- | --- | --- |
| Equities | Common stock<br>Preferred stock<br>Rights<br>Warrants | • Reference data<br>• Multiple identifier types<br>• Security descriptive data<br>• Pricing and derived data<br>• Corporate actions<br>• Issuer data |
| Debt/fixed income | Corporate<br>Government<br>Agency<br>Municipal<br>Structured products<br>Floating rate notes | • Reference data<br>• Multiple identifier types<br>• Security descriptive data<br>• Pricing and derived data<br>• Terms and conditions<br>• Issuer data |
| Derivatives | Options<br>Futures | • Reference data<br>• Descriptive data<br>• Pricing and derived data<br>• Underlying instruments/<br>constituents<br>• Corporate actions |
| Money market | Foreign exchange, spot<br>Foreign exchange,<br>  forwards<br>Deposits<br>Interbank rates<br>Commercial paper<br>Bankers acceptances<br>Swaps | • Reference data<br>• Pricing and derived data<br>such as yields<br>• Underlying benchmarks |
| Collective<br>  investments/funds | Mutual funds<br>Unit investment trusts<br>Money market funds<br>Exchange traded funds | • Reference data<br>• Pricing and related derived data<br>• Collective investment details<br>• Constituents and weightings<br>• Corporate actions |
| Indices | Exchanges<br>Agencies<br>Bonds<br>Geographic markets | • Reference data<br>• Multiple identifier types<br>• Pricing and related derived data<br>• Constituents and weightings |

The primary key to all asset class entities is the **instrument identifier**, as described in Chapter 3. Typically, however, no one security identifier can meet the needs of any one firm. The geographic nature of clearing codes and market nature of ticker symbols and other codes presents a major obstacle to meeting these needs.

As a result, the concept of cross-referencing security identifiers needs to be considered as part of any framework for describing capital markets data. Within this guide, cross-referencing is supported as a reference data subclass, as described in Chapter 3.

## Security classification schemes

The nice thing about standards, as the saying goes, is that there are so many of them!

This little maxim, no doubt familiar to most market data professionals, has no greater relevance than when discussing security classification schemes. There are several to choose from, sometimes all provided as part of the same datafeed service.

This diversity has typically arisen out of necessity. Data suppliers need to provide their customers with categorization information for the securities they deliver. As such, major vendors have all been forced to create and manage their own schemes – which, of course, don't reconcile with their competitors' classification schemes.

The problem then gets much worse. Independent agencies as well as bodies such as the International Standards Organization (ISO) have all produced a variety of additional classification schemes. For many of the same reasons, a number of financial firms have adopted their own in-house versions. And, of course, even this guide adds to the mess, with the very basic asset classification scheme that is a fundamental component to this logical framework.

The result is pretty chaotic as, almost by definition, none of these schemes fully reconciles with any of the others. To date, there is no single standard adopted across the industry for the classification of securities. As a result, many data vendors provide multiple schemes, including their own, as part of their information services. The result is a fair degree of complexity in trying to reconcile classification of securities across data sources.

From the point of view of laying out a general framework for such a key element of capital markets data, this presents a bit of a problem. In order to be truly useful, financial instruments do need to be classified, after all. However, not only do many of the schemes in use today overlap (thereby duplicating content for all intents and purposes); they also offer varying degrees of precision based on various asset classes.

The good news is that global standards are being set and are being adopted, albeit not as quickly as would be useful. Therefore, there remains only one option for this framework – to support any security classification within the same logical structure.

The key point to recognize here is that a classification scheme must always be associated with each and every classification value. Taking this approach allows for multiple schemes to be associated with any one instrument. This is important, as it couples the type of classification scheme tightly to the specific values. This reflects the need for a user of this content to define the classification scheme in use. Again, in today's markets it is entirely likely that no one classification scheme will be in use firm-wide (and certainly not across the industry). Therefore, the only remaining option is to identify the scheme type in use with the actual data content.

### Third-party information

Associated with all securities are a number of directly related service providers. In many cases, these third parties have a direct impact on the valuation of the security and how it can be transacted between counterparties. Examples of third parties include:

- Lead manager/underwriter
- Co-manager
- Trustee
- Counsel
- Paying agent
- Re-marketing agent
- Tender agent
- Transfer agent
- Registrar
- Escrow agent
- Financial advisor
- Clearing agent
- Information agent.

Many data services include at least some record of various third parties associated with a particular financial instrument or issuer. There is, however, no single predetermined universe of coverage. While for some business applications (such as trading or research) identification of third parties is not vital, for others (such as custody or accounts payable) it may be absolutely essential.

For the most part, third-party information does not impact directly on the value of a security. It is more related to operational functions that follow from transactions. As the list above shows, there are quite a number of third parties that can be relevant – and therefore extensibility is an important consideration when looking at this content type.

The most important factor to note is that third parties are represented as a name/type pair. In this way, any third-party service provider can be supported as part of the framework. Secondly, third-party information is linked to the framework through the use of the **instrument identifier** or **issuer identifier**, allowing for either the security or corporate level to be handled.

### Conversion terms

Some securities include features that allow them to convert into other securities as part of their defining terms. The most common form of conversion is typically fixed income instruments converting into preferred equity instruments (and *vice versa*).

Convertible securities are popular investments, as the conversion features provide a built-in risk management feature for investors. Indeed, convertible arbitrage is a very well-used investment strategy in today's capital markets. While not without risk, it does have a strong track record of results.

From the data perspective, convertible securities fit naturally into the framework. As one of the primary goals is to provide a consolidated cross-asset view of capital markets information, supporting a data type that records conversions makes perfect sense, leveraging the depth of coverage supported for the individual asset classes on either side. Since this is by definition a cross-asset function, the conversion terms data subtype is considered as part of the global business data universe.

The conversion terms subtype is structured around three principal concepts:

1. *Conversion terms* – providing details related to the terms under which the conversion can be exercised. This information is typically sourced from a prospectus or similar document

2. *Conversion events* – providing a historical record of when conversions occur, as well as recording the schedule on when they may take place in future

3. *Conversion details* – additional information (typically in free-form text) associated with a particular event.

It is worth taking special note of the logic applied here, as it is central to much of the asset-specific data subtype described in Chapter 5.

When looking at financial instruments, there are three key items to recognize that dictate much of the related data content that is produced by the capital markets:

1. *Terms* – defining characteristics that are documented in the prospectus or other contract underlying the instrument. All financial instruments have legal terms under which they are created and marketed

2. *Events* – records of specific *terms* of the instrument that are or can be invoked by either the issuer or the buyer of the security. Events can happen both on a scheduled

basis and in response to specific business developments (which are quite often classified as *corporate actions*, described later in this chapter)

3. *Details* – these provide information specifically relating to an *event*.

Taken together, these three logical entities – as illustrated for conversion terms above – provide a consistent manner in which to consider the features and actions that can be associated with a complex financial security. This logic is central to the general framework, and is re-used across many of the asset-specific data subtypes described in the following sections. This is a good example of the benefits of laying out a logical framework for market data, as it takes advantage of the same, consistent concepts to represent relatively complex concepts.

## TRADING DATA

By definition, all financial market instruments are traded between buyers and sellers (collectively referred to as 'counterparties'). The act of trading is the means by which the economic value and liquidity of the instrument is measured. As a result, the data produced from trading activity, called here *trading data*, is common to all financial instruments and can therefore be represented within a single data subtype.

Trading data is by definition related to the market level of the logical framework. Before any instrument can be exchanged between counterparties it must exist in at least one market, such as an exchange.

An important point to recognize here is not to confuse an exchange with a market. It is very common to encounter no distinction between the two terms when working with capital markets data, even to the point of seeing them used interchangeably within datafeed documentation. While the differences between the two may appear semantic, they are significant.

Exchanges are a type of market where instruments are formally listed, requiring issuers to operate in a certain, regulated manner. Financial instruments can also be traded over the counter, with little or no involvement of an exchange (quite often, trades conducted off-market are reported to exchanges as a part of regulatory and other requirements). So not all transactions occur on exchanges. However, the same instrument is still quoted in one or more markets.

Trading data easily represents the greatest volume of capital markets data encountered on a daily basis. As securities typically trade daily, there is a constant stream of expressions to buy or sell securities, all expressed as realtime quotes over a variety of services. Trading data is by definition created by the results of active trading. It is reported in realtime (i.e. 'tick by tick') by exchanges and other sources, and is closely followed. Numerous vendor firms consolidate these electronic feeds and deliver them to market participants via a variety of sophisticated applications.

For the purposes of this guide, this content set is grouped into the following logical subtypes:

1. *Pricing data* – attributes that indicate the economic value placed on an individual security by participants in the market. A host of factors affect the value, ranging across the content described here. Pricing data has two subtypes:
   - end of day – pricing values recorded at the end of day to provide a benchmark for a variety of functions
   - time and sales – time-indexed records of pricing values and counterparties recorded over the course of the trading day
2. *Time and sales data* – at the most specific level are details related to each individual trade, recording the time of the transaction and the details related to the sale (block size, execution price, bid and ask prices at time of execution, etc.)
3. *Aggregated data* – much data is aggregated and calculated across the market. Examples include indices, total volume, number of advancers and decliners, etc.
4. *Market rules* – information that describes the manner in which the market operates and the conventions that are followed.

Figure 4.4 lays out the logical representation of these subtypes and their integration within the general framework.

Details on each of these logical entities is given in the following sections.

## Pricing data

This trading data subtype represents by far the largest collection of information. As mentioned previously, it is created and distributed in realtime as a result of buyers and sellers expressing indications of interest, and therefore represents a significant volume produced each and every trading day.

Within this framework, pricing data is divided into two separate subtypes:

1. End of day
2. Time and sales.

The two are closely related, as they contain pretty much the same universe of attributes. The difference is that the former is built around the concept of a single day-end value used principally for post-trade, operational functions as well as in time-based statistical analysis. The latter is more commonly used for front-office analytical functions, as it presents a record of all transactions occurring within a given market over the course of the trading day.

The fundamental difference between the two boils down to volume. On its own, end-of-day pricing data produces, on a global basis, over three million pricing records

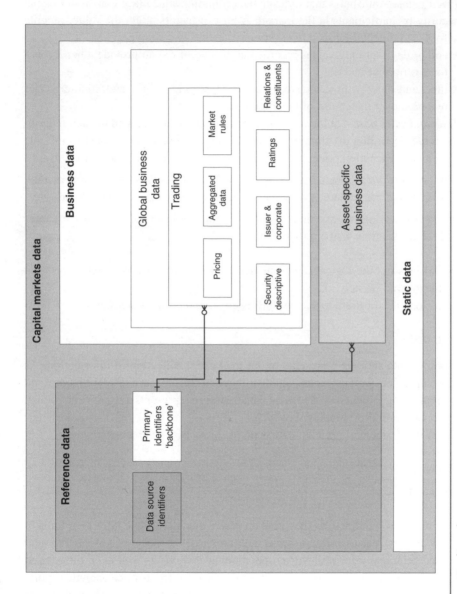

**Figure 4.4** Trading data.

containing on average ten pricing facts (at least) each and every trading day. Time and sales records for each of these instruments represents several orders of magnitude greater volume. Obviously, while operating a global database of securities populated with day-end pricing is feasible, to do the same thing for time and sales records represents a completely different challenge.

A second key difference is quality control. Realtime streaming data typically doesn't worry too much about quality control – pricing records are overwritten with the next quote, so timeliness of delivery usually outweighs accuracy of values. Indeed, market participants watching these streams are well versed in picking out erroneous values, and vendors do provide automated quality control which also helps. When archived to a historical record, such as a time and sales log, however, such discrepancies stand out and are likely to cause problems in analysis.

For end-of-day values, though, such discrepancies are not acceptable. Consequently, vendors invest heavily in ensuring the accuracy of the content, as these values are used to provide a snapshot view of the economic value of securities for historical analytical purposes. As a result, simply ignoring odd values is not a feasible solution as it is for realtime data and, to a lesser extent, the associated time and sales records.

### End-of-day pricing

At the end of the trading day, pricing data is also fundamental to a wide set of other business applications – including clearing, settlement, accounting and risk management, to name but a few. These are none other than the end-of-day values collected from the realtime stream at the appropriate time every day. Ultimately, these values are then used in pre-trade functions such as research and decision support.

This realtime-to-archived relationship is important to understand. It underpins the fundamental assertion in this guide that there should be no distinction placed on 'realtime' versus 'reference' data. It is all the same content; the only difference is the frequency with which it updates. Indeed, treating the two as different and unrelated forms of content will almost certainly lead to disconnects between a firm's trading and other operational functions.

The pricing data subtype is made up of the following attributes:

1. *Trade facts* – the universe of statistical facts that are used to communicate the value of the security. Examples include (and are certainly not limited to):
   - open price
   - high price
   - low price
   - bid price
   - ask price

- last price
- close price
- volume

2. *Trade value* – the actual observed value for the associated trade fact
3. *Date* – all pricing data is date-relevant
4. *Time* – the time of day at which a trade value was produced
5. *Frequency* – the periodicity on which the trade values are collected. Examples include:
   - tick-by-tick
   - daily
   - weekly
   - monthly
   - quarterly
   - yearly
6. *Price type* – the convention, if any, under which the price is quoted. Examples include:
   - nominal, as reported
   - quoted with interest
   - etc. etc.

More complete definitions for each of these attributes are given in the data dictionary in Chapter 6.

For realtime applications, this content is pretty much one-dimensional. The application simply displays the latest value received from the datafeed, giving the user a direct connection to activities in the market. Historical sets of this content may be used to support the buy/sell decision process (by supporting historical charts for example) but, by and large, once a value receives an update it is removed from the application.

Reference data applications, however, tend to maintain large historical stores of pricing data content. This content is indexed based on date (for daily data) and/or time (for time and sales data – see next section). The descriptive jargon for this content is referred to as 'timeseries'.

### Time and sales

This subtype is a specialized form of trading data. It provides a log of the transactions for securities traded on a given day. It is therefore historical information, and is used primarily for analytical and related purposes.

It should be noted that the time and sales data type references the same trade facts as trading. As such, it needs to exist in only one location, despite the fact that this is a different subtype within the market data type.

## Aggregated data

The financial markets would not be the same without the use of aggregated or calculated statistical values. Examples of these values include:

- Total market volume
- Total market turnover
- Number of advancing securities
- Number of declining securities
- Number unchanged
- Number of trades executed.

One option for representing these types of values would be simply to treat them as additional trade facts. However, as these values are derived from actual trade values which represent an actual value reported to the markets, this would be to violate some of the fundamental logic.

As an alternative, these values are grouped together as market statistics. In this way, this derived content is kept separate from the actual market-generated content but is accessible in precisely the same manner, providing a consistent way in which to navigate this content.

## Market rules

The last trading data subtype is the rules and conventions under which the market operates. This information can be relatively hard to acquire, yet is fundamental to many applications for market data. Some vendors do publish this content to varying degrees of accuracy, but to date there is no single global standard adopted across the industry. As a result, financial firms are forced to track these rules independently – which may not be difficult when operating in domestic markets, but presents non-trivial (and annoying) challenges when operating in foreign markets.

The information making up this subtype is relatively static and doesn't change too frequently. With several hundred exchanges in the world alone, however, even a small number of changes published periodically can have a negative impact. Attributes making up this subtype include:

- Trading calendars – details on when the market operates, including the days of the week and times of day
- Holiday calendars – a predetermined schedule of non-trading days outside of the regularly scheduled trading calendar

■ Settlement conventions – rules by which securities transactions must be completed through to full exchange and accounting (Settlement varies by instrument type and geography)

■ Regulatory details – rules and conventions mandated by regulators of individual markets.

## RATINGS

The value of publicly traded financial instruments is directly affected, sometimes violently, by evaluations issued by rating agencies. These ratings are issued at two levels:

1.  *Security* – evaluation of the security (primarily fixed income) and associated risk of default in servicing the payment stream
2.  *Corporate* – an assessment of the creditworthiness of the issuer.

As ratings information relates to both the instrument and issuer levels, it qualifies as a global business data type.

Like security classifications schemes, there is a wide diversity of agencies that research and monitor securities and issue ratings. Some of the better-known firms include Standard & Poor's, Moody's, and Fitch.

Like security classifications, each source has its own logical structure regarding ratings. Therefore, the logical representation within the framework is relatively similar. Consistency in representation is an important factor in making the framework easy to use. This logic is captured in Figure 4.5.

Each agency uses a proprietary schema for evaluating securities and corporations. The following subsections give details on how these schemas are supported for both instruments and issuers within the framework.

### Instrument ratings

A key attribute associated with many securities is the ratings issued by independent agencies. These ratings values are extremely important and are closely followed by the investment community. Changes in ratings can dramatically influence the value that investors are willing to pay.

As illustrated in Figure 4.5, an individual security, as identified by its instrument identifier, can have one or more (optional) ratings associated with it. Each rating in turn is associated with a rating agency. As with security classification schemes, this allows for easy selection of the required rating types.

In addition to rendering the ratings as reported by one or more agencies, the securities ratings type also includes the concept of additional details related to a rating and ratings events.

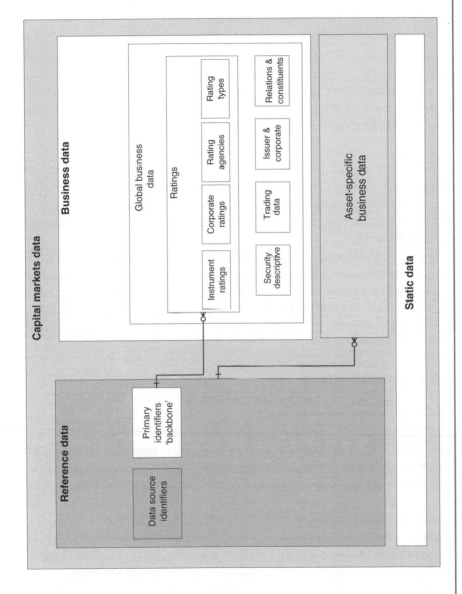

**Figure 4.5** Ratings information.

An important element of the ratings entity is the rating type. This field allows for multiple forms of ratings-related information to be associated with any one security. These include:

- The actual rating as issued by the various agencies
- Whether the security has been placed on a watchlist
- Reviewed ratings.

As such, this framework provides an extensible means in which new ratings-related information can be added. With many firms providing ratings and more likely to enter the market, extensibility and flexibility are important features.

### Issuer ratings

Issuer ratings are handled in precisely the same manner as security ratings. The issuer identifier provides the primary key to identify the issuer. All issuer ratings are provided in the corporate ratings table. In turn, both the corporate and security ratings share the same static data.

By splitting the universe of ratings into two entities – corporate ratings and security ratings – the volume of content is minimized, supporting high-performance querying. Performance considerations are particularly relevant as ratings information is used across a number of different query types, ranging from the straightforward to the very complex.

## ISSUER & CORPORATE DATA

All financial instruments have an issuer of one type or another. The entity that produces the instrument is a fundamental attribute of capital markets data content, either directly (as in an equity issue) or at arm's length (as in derivative contracts). As it reflects information concerning the issuing organization, it is common across the entire data framework and is therefore classified as part of the global business data subclass.

The issuer & corporate data type provides details that are related to corporate organizations (including companies, government, multilateral agencies and so on). In general, corporate data is associated with a relatively low frequency of update. Changes are typically issued on a quarterly or annual basis, reflecting the reporting periods associated with corporate organizations. However, corporate data is also relatively event-sensitive. Changes impacting on management and other activities can result in announcements that affect security prices, credit ratings and, ultimately, yields to holders.

The key categories of data making up this data type are:

1. *Issuer details* – basic information that identifies the corporate entity, such as name, country of headquarters, etc.
2. *Performance data* – actual and forecast data measuring the issuer's business operations. Performance data is made up of the following subtypes:
   - balance sheets
   - cash flow statements
   - income statements
   - corporate financial ratios
3. *Industry classifications* – these identify the industry sectors and subsectors to which a corporate entity is associated. There is a variety of industry classifications used in the industry
4. *Ownership hierarchies* – details on the ownership of the corporate entity and related security to legal entity relationships.

By definition, the primary key for all related content is the **corporate identifier**, as described in Chapter 2. Navigation to corporate-level business data is via the issuer entity, as illustrated in Figure 4.6.

Each of the constituent subtypes is described in the following sections.

## Issuer details

This subtype provides the general descriptive information associated with corporate entities. A variety of information falls into this category, including:

- Corporate names (both primary and alternate names)
- Geographic incorporation
- Address details
- Key personnel.

Taken as a whole, this subtype provides the basic information needed to define an issuer.

## Performance data

Widely followed in the industry for analysis purposes and closely monitored by the press, this subtype provides measures of an issuer's business activity and overall health over a given period. As a result, this is of direct interest to investors and potential investors.

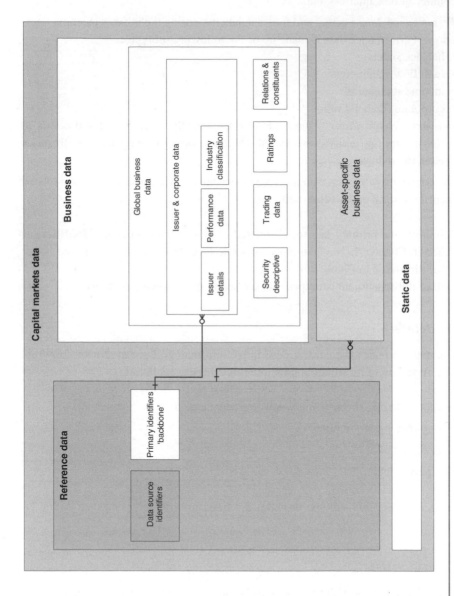

**Figure 4.6** Corporate and fundamental data.

By and large, the data making up this subtype is based on accounting information. Public companies must report their performance at predetermined frequency (typically quarterly and annual), thereby providing shareholders and other investors with a current snapshot of the firm's financial health.

There are four key groups of information that are common across all firms:

1. Balance sheets
2. Cash flow statements
3. Income statements
4. Financial ratios.

A key objective of this guide is to provide a single coherent structure for the representation of financial data. This principle is challenged when it comes to corporate performance data, as there is a variety of accounting standards in use around the world. From the data perspective, this problem manifests itself as a fair degree of diversity in how the information is delivered by vendors and other data sources.

### Balance sheets
Balance sheets reflect a company's net worth (value of assets less value of liabilities) at a given point in time, and therefore are extremely important in assessing credit- and investment-worthiness. The balance sheet entity shown in Figure 4.6 is joined to the backbone of the framework via the issuer entity. It contains a series of attributes that reflect the most commonly cited items used in investment research and other functions.

Over and above the attributes provided in the balance sheet entity, there is typically significant additional detail available. This is largely grouped around the following subtypes:

1. *Asset details* – representing the financial value of what the firm owns
2. *Liabilities* – legal financial obligations that the firm holds
3. *Issuer equity* – representing the amount of funds contributed by the owners of the firm (i.e. shareholders) plus any retained earnings (or losses)
4. *Reserves* – cash and other cash-like securities that are held in reserve against future liabilities or other obligations
5. *Investments* – reflecting the value of money invested elsewhere and the associated rate of return (or lack thereof), which affects the net worth of the firm.

### Cash flows
Cash flow statements provide details on the company's ability to generate net cash to run and reinvest in the business. In many cases, the cash flow provides an early indication of the firm's pending performance.

The cash flow entity shown in Figure 4.6 provides the gateway to accessing this information. The issuer identifier provides the link between cash flow and the backbone via the issuer entity, integrating to the full framework.

There are two detailed cash flow subtypes that should be considered:

1. *Financing* – making available details on any capital-raising activities providing the company with additional cash resources
2. *Cash flow details* – capturing specific events that impact on the cash generation.

## Income statements

Also known as the 'profit and loss' or 'P&L' statement, the income statement is a company financial report that summarizes the revenues and expenses incurred by a firm during a specific accounting period. It provides an indication of the firm's financial performance resulting from ongoing business operations.

The income statement entity also provides the gateway to two further areas of detail:

1. *Revenue details* – providing details on all revenues received over the course of the accounting period
2. *Expense details* – detailing the outlays that were recorded in the period.

By separating these details from the higher-level, more standard information, the framework provides a means by which the complexities associated with any one issuer are addressed.

## Financial ratios

In order to measure corporate performance, analysts typically produce derived, calculated values. In turn, these values can be used to assess performance within a portfolio or against industry benchmarks.

The universe of financial ratios is very large and very diverse, reflecting both geographic as well as industry-specific analysis requirements. Within the logical framework, this complexity is represented as a simple name/value pair consisting of:

- Ratio type – indicating the derived value
- Ratio value – the published value associated with the ratio type.

As with all other corporate performance data, this construct allows for the full breadth of coverage as well as extensibility. From the analyst's perspective, coupling the ratio type to the ratio value is essential. Hence, representation in this fashion within the framework is consistent with business application.

## *Industry classifications*

The financial services industry makes use of a variety of classification schemes for identifying the industry to which a corporation entity belongs. Many investment strategies, for example, are sector-based, requiring the use of an industry classification scheme.

Unfortunately, industry classification is a subject area that suffers from much the same challenges as security classifications, discussed earlier. There are many different schemes used across the industry and globally. And, just like security classifications, there is no concordance across these classifications. Examples of such schemes include:

- Standard Industrial Classification (SIC)
- Morgan Stanley Capital International (MSCI)
- GICS
- Dow Jones STOXX Industrial Classification
- ICB Benchmark (FTSE/Dow Jones).

In addition, data vendors themselves publish their own proprietary schemes as well. As a result, there is a wide diversity in classification schemes in use across the industry, and no standard is yet considered as fully accepted.

From the point of view of a data user, this complexity and lack of a globally accepted standard can be immensely frustrating. In order to represent this diverse content within a single content, precisely the same logic as supported for security classifications is used.

The benefits of this approach are the same as for securities. By coupling the scheme type with the individual issuer, all classification values associated with that issuer can be referenced at the same time. While not providing an actual concordance between the schemes, it does make it much easier to see the various values alongside one another for comparison purposes (assuming they exist, of course).

## RELATIONS AND CONSTITUENTS

One of the more complex characteristics of market data at all three levels of the logical hierarchy is that one item is related quite closely to one or more other items. In some cases, such as investment funds and indices, this characteristic is fundamental to individual instruments. These relationships occur at two levels:

1. *Issuer level* – identifying corporate ownership and holdings
2. *Instrument level* – providing records of constituents & weightings.

The data produced for this universe is relatively complex and is published by some of the more specialized data vendors. Within the logical framework, this content takes the form shown in Figure 4.7.

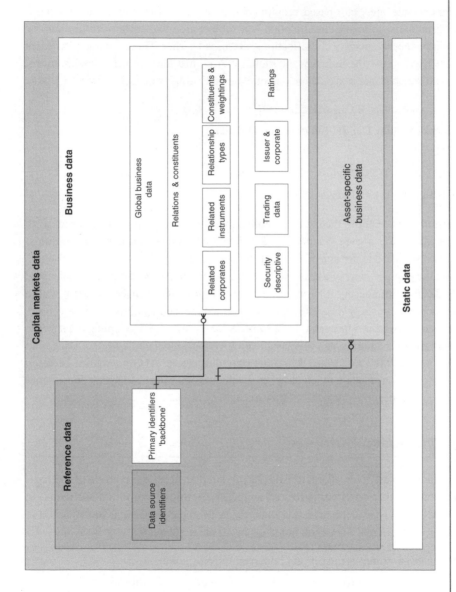

**Figure 4.7** Relations and constituents.

As Figure 4.7 shows, the subtype is used for a number of purposes within the framework. As such it is considered as one of the global business data types.

## Corporate ownership and holdings

Many corporate entities (and corporations in particular) are owned in whole or in part by other entities. As a result, understanding the ownership structure to which a particular entity is exposed is an important factor in calculating the risk associated with the securities issued by the corporation.

This guide treats ownership in the same manner as constituent securities. The relations/constituents data type described in the next section provides a means for handling both, as illustrated in Figure 4.7.

The relationships shown demonstrate that the logical nature of ownership or holdings is relatively straightforward. Any given issuer, identified by an issuer identifier, can have an interest in any other related corporate entity. The relationship type then serves to define precisely the nature of this relationship. Examples include:

■ Wholly owned subsidiary
■ Minority interest
■ Joint venture.

## Security relations/constituents & weightings

A common characteristic of financial instruments and other statistics is that they are made up of a combination of underlying instruments. This applies to the following asset classes and data types:

■ Funds – mutual funds, unit investment trusts, money market funds, etc. are all collective items comprised of a number of underlying instruments making up a portfolio. The membership of the portfolio, along with the weight of the individual component in the portfolio (adding up to 100 per cent), is recorded

■ Indices – the components of a particular index, such as Standard & Poor's 500 (S&P500), on a given date. This information is essential for investment managers who manage portfolios based on the market index

■ Basket securities – composite securities, such as an exchange-traded fund or privately managed portfolio.

The relations/constituents data type provides a means of representing the universe of underlying or related instruments making up the composite group. Figure 4.7 lays out how this subtype is supported.

A key point to note here is that this data subtype supports both the corporate- and security-level relations. More importantly, they both use the same logical structure and attributes. While this does imply elements of duplication within the framework, the fundamental corporate-to-security relationship makes this a necessity. In this way, the data content relevant to the issuer level doesn't get mixed up with the instrument-level information.

## Asset-specific business data

Not all business data types are global in nature, as the content in question is specialized to one or more asset types. This is an important characteristic of capital markets data, as not all attributes apply to all instruments. From the point of view of implementing applications that use this data, such an approach would be very inefficient and unnecessarily complex. As a result, reducing the universe of data content to that which is relevant to a particular asset class or subclass is an effective way of making navigating the complex content as straightforward as possible.

As outlined in Chapter 2, this framework is built around the cross-reference between asset classes and data types. For the most part, this cross-reference is kept to the asset class level, in an effort to make the drill-down to the actual business data content a consistent exercise.

Some of the most complex and, from the point of view of a user of capital markets data, intimidating business data content falls into the asset-specific data type. This reflects the nature of the information itself, which tends to increase in complexity in response to the sophistication of the security. The data subtypes defined within this framework are:

1. *Corporate actions* – business events and announcements that have a material impact on holders of the associated financial instruments
2. *Terms & conditions* – the defining legal terms, events and details associated with securities (primarily fixed income)
3. *Payment information* – contracted terms, events and details associated with the income stream associated with securities
4. *Collective investment details* – this covers the information related to securities, such as mutual funds, that are made up of other securities
5. *Clearing information* – information related to the clearing and settlement rules associated with securities
6. *Tax information* – details on the tax treatment related to securities.

To a greater or lesser degree, data vendors make elements of these content sets available as part of their services. In addition, specialist vendors provide services that provide additional levels of detail related to these highly specified subtypes. In order to be useful to financial firms, then, this information needs to be integrated across data sources.

The framework presented by this guide provides one means by which this integration can be undertaken, at least at a logical level, as illustrated in Figure 4.8.

It's important to note here how these subtypes integrate with the wider framework. The data types integrate either at the point of specific asset class (terms & conditions) or at the general instrument level (payment, tax, corporate actions, clearing). This provides a quick way in which to identify the general nature of the constituent information within the data subtype – where the content is specific to a subtype, it integrates to the asset class only; where it is more generally applied, it integrates to the instrument level.

Detailed descriptions of the various components making up each of these subclasses are given in the following sections.

## CORPORATE ACTIONS

One of the recurring themes in this guide is the lack of precise definition in the industry for certain broadly used terms. Perhaps nowhere is the fallout from this assumed mutual understanding more severe than when it comes to corporate actions. Ask any two practitioners in the industry, and there are likely to be five or more different definitions of the term!

The traditionally accepted definition used in the industry defines corporate actions as the act of a publicly traded company initiating a process that will affect its issued securities. These events affect the capital structure of the company, and can significantly affect very important items such as pricing and cash flows. Examples of corporate actions include:

1. *Dividends* – logical records that describe the declaration of dividends as business events. Each dividend announcement for a given equity security has a unique event identifier, allowing for subsequent updates to be supported as additional information becomes available

2. *Capital changes* – providing logical records of changes to the capital structure that typically affect an investor's holdings. Examples include splits, reverse splits and dilutions (by, for example, the exercise of rights, etc.)

3. *Earnings* – logical records of earnings announcements

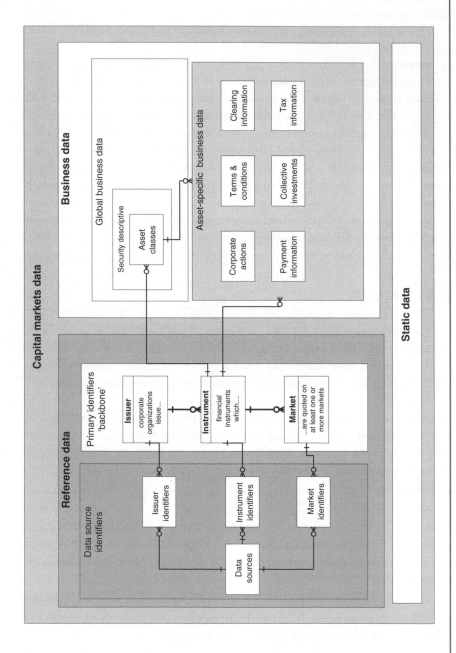

**Figure 4.8**   Asset-specific business data types.

4. *Shares outstanding* – details regarding the number of shares outstanding, as identified by the primary key (and its associated relationship to market identifiers), of a particular security

5. *Reorganization notices* – many other corporate actions events are reported under this general heading. This subtype within the corporate actions data type provides detailed textual based records describing the events in detail.

To be sure, these events all result in a significant number of corporate actions announcements – so simply redefining the term will likely not resolve the business problem.

Under the traditional definition, corporate actions information is primarily of interest to back-office and other operational functions. This is because corporate actions announcements affect the structure of the underlying instrument, requiring administration to ensure that such changes are accurately reflected in the accounts where such instruments are held.

However, the reality of today's business environment is that such a definition is too restricted. This is because, whether or not firms admit it, corporate actions information is used in many more applications than is generally recognized. Indeed, as the announcement of corporate actions information can result in significant changes to prices, the sooner it can be delivered across the enterprise the better.

Ultimately, the question of what constitutes a corporate actions announcement, then, is context-sensitive and very dependent on the application of the data itself. As capital markets have grown significantly and introduced increasingly complex financial instruments, the use of the term has continued to expand. Obviously, such a situation can easily lead to miscommunication both within and between firms, resulting in processing interruptions and other costly problems. So a more robust definition is clearly needed.

The fundamental, defining attribute of corporate actions is that it represents a change that may potentially affect the value of a security held by an investor. Looking at corporate actions from this point of view, then, leads to a particularly interesting observation – *in theory, any modification to a non-trading data attribute (as defined within this framework at least) could be considered to be a corporate action.*

The definition explicitly excludes pricing data. This is because pricing, by its very nature, changes on a fixed basis, and is therefore recurring, not event-based.

Viewed from this perspective, then, corporate actions can be classified into three separate categories:

1. Announcements related to the exercising of terms of a security
2. Announcements that terms of a security will not be met
3. Announcements that affect a security at arm's length.

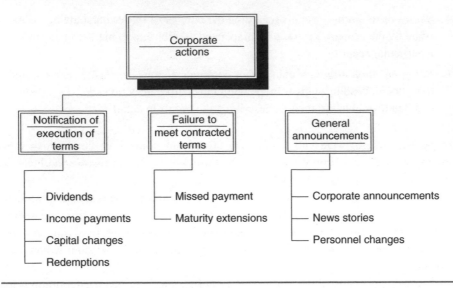

**Figure 4.9**   Corporate actions data.

Looking at these three subtypes (shown in Figure 4.9) with some corresponding examples provides a better understanding.

The three general categories presented above reflect the importance of the announcement types:

1. Announcements related to the exercising of terms of a security are typically well understood and in many cases are anticipated. Therefore, the administration and notification requirements are relatively well understood. Examples include:
   • dividend announcements
   • capital change announcements (splits, dilution, etc.)
   • shares outstanding changes
   • payments as per the prospectus (e.g. coupon payments)
   • redemptions
2. Announcements that terms of a security will not be met typically impact on the value of the instrument. This in turn impacts on the yield to the holder (which can go to a complete write-off of the investment in the case of bankruptcy). Examples include:
   • missed coupon payments
   • accruals of missed payments
   • maturity extensions
3. Announcements that affect a security at arm's length involve routine information about the issuer and/or the security which provide additional news. While the

announcement does not impact the security directly, the event itself can cause a change in the security's value. Examples include:

- name changes
- merger announcements
- security symbol changes
- reorganization events.

From the point of a view of a logical framework, these three subtypes take the form shown in Figure 4.10.

Ultimately, the most important point to note about corporate actions is that they convey notices of change. The impact of these announcements varies by business functions. For many uses, an up-to-date record of all notices is important. For others, only those changes that have a related financial impact are relevant.

Such diversity of uses for this content argues for a very broad-based approach to structuring the content. Within this framework, then, corporate actions can be thought of as modification to any attribute outside of the trading data subtype. By monitoring these attributes for changes, classified as described above, users of the content can decide whether or not a particular modification is useful.

More importantly, though, thinking of corporate actions along these lines ensures that no announcements are missed. This is doubly important, as such announcements are made as updates to fields published by data sources. Thus, by monitoring individual attributes, the business application can decide as to whether or not the change is of value.

At a more detailed level, Figure 4.10 identifies three absolutely key attributes in dealing with corporate actions:

1. *Corporate actions event identifier* – a value that uniquely identifies a corporate action announcement. By their very nature, these announcements are delivered on a time-based, interim basis. Most announcements are initiated with an initial high-level declaration followed by several updates that add details as they become finalized. With a unique identifier, each announcement can be considered as a separate event, to which subsequent updates with additional detail are provided. This approach provides a complete audit trail associated with each event

2. *Corporate actions event type* – a value that defines the nature of the event. Unfortunately, no single definition of event types is adopted by the industry. As such, data users are pretty much constrained by the content provided by their datafeed services, which tends to be closer to the traditional definition

3. *Announcement date* – the date on which the corporate action event was declared. This is very useful, as it identifies the point at which the process was begun and affects a number of resulting date types, including record date, pay date and ex-date (if appropriate).

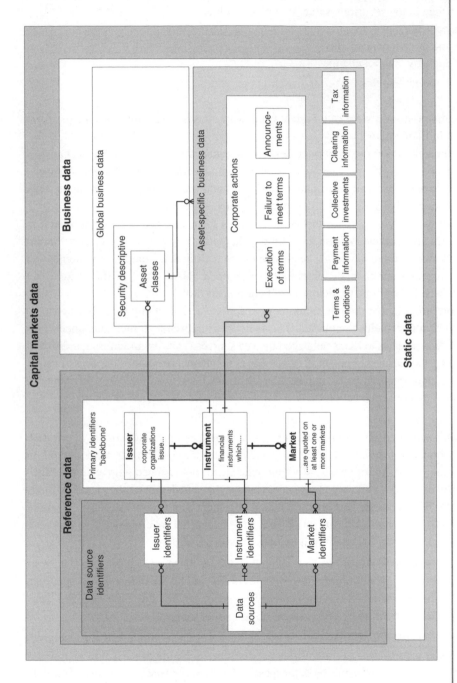

**Figure 4.10** Corporate actions and the framework.

## TERMS & CONDITIONS

Primarily associated with fixed income instruments, this data type contains details on the legal structure of securities, the conditions under which they may be exercised, and related historical records of the events. The original source for much of this content is the prospectus associated with the security, and subsequent announcements made by the issuer.

Terms & conditions content is quite large and very diverse, reflecting the sophistication of fixed income securities and the very broad trading that occurs. From the perspective of a logical framework, the data content breaks down into the following broad subtypes:

1. *Summary information* – broadly common information that describes the general characteristics of the fixed income security

2. *Redemption information* – many fixed income securities include provisions for the issuer or the holder to redeem the security on predefined terms and schedules

3. *Floating rate notes* – this subtype provides full details regarding securities that have the ability to change the coupon payable to the bond holder

4. *Sinking funds* – provides details regarding the terms and schedules under which the issuer of the security can provide funds against the repayment of the debt

5. *Municipal bonds* – this category of bonds has additional specific details over and above standard terms & conditions

6. *Structured products* – provides additional details to the specialized instrument types of Collateralized Mortgage Obligations (CMO), Mortgage Backed Bonds (MBS) and other Asset Backed Securities (ABS).

Figure 4.11 illustrates the logical structure used in the framework.

Introduced earlier, as part of the discussion regarding the conversion terms data subtype with security descriptive data, terms & conditions data is structured around three fundamental concepts:

1. *Terms* – information sourced directly from the prospectus of the security. These are the legal conditions that define the security

2. *Details* – additional information that describes further the terms and conditions under which the security is issued

3. *Events* – a time-based record (either historical or looking into the future) where a term of the bond has been invoked by either the issuer or the holder of the bond.

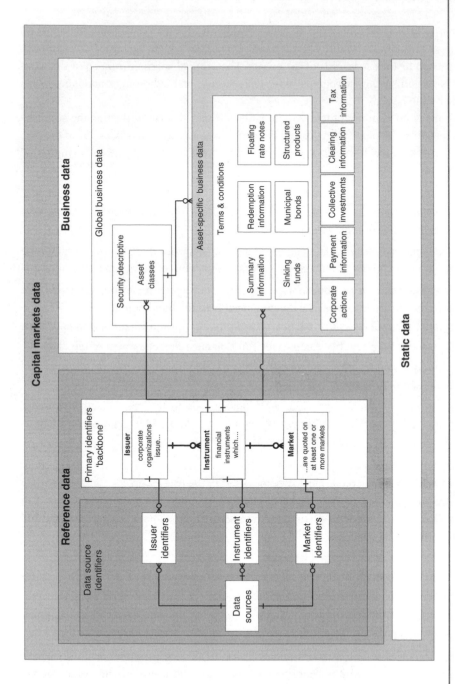

**Figure 4.11** Terms & conditions data.

**Table 4.2**   Terms and conditions cross-reference.

|  | Terms | Details | Events |
|---|---|---|---|
| Summary information | ✔ | ✔ | |
| Redemption information | ✔ | ✔ | ✔ |
| Floating rate notes | ✔ | ✔ | ✔ |
| Sinking funds | ✔ | ✔ | ✔ |
| Municipal bonds | ✔ | ✔ | |
| Structured products | ✔ | ✔ | |

Table 4.2 provides a cross-reference between the subtypes making up terms & conditions and each of these categories.

Details on each of these terms & conditions subtypes are provided in the following subsections.

First, though, it's worth touching on the relationship between terms & conditions and corporate actions described in the previous section. Since terms & conditions represent such a large domain of attributes (typically almost half by most counts of data sources), it represents a rich source of corporate actions information as defined within the scope of this framework. Furthermore, as bonds and other fixed income instruments are marketed as a means of locking in predictable cash flow with low risk to the holder, changes to specific terms can have an immediate financial impact.

It should be noted that this is a two-way relationship. Where a regularly scheduled commitment, such as a coupon payment, is not honored (for whatever reason), then this too can be considered a corporate action event. Obviously, a missed interest payment directly impacts the holder of the security.

Corporate actions and terms & conditions are treated as separate subtypes within this framework. As a result, some duplication of content (i.e. 'denormalization') is possible. The two, however, do not conflict, as corporate actions provides a means of tracking specified events (assuming they are considered as valid corporate actions subtypes) that are defined in detail by the terms & conditions subtype. Combined, they provide complete details on the event.

### Summary information

This subtype of data within terms & conditions refers to the most common data elements used by applications and supported to a lesser or greater extent across major market data vendors. The content is standardized as it is loaded into the database and is presented in common fashion, regardless of the data source.

The entities making up this subclass are:

■ Bond details – contain generic information regarding the instrument; this entity also serves as the linkage point to the more detailed, vendor-specific data described below

■ Issuance – information related to the initial issue event of the security covering underwriting, over allotment provisions and other related details

■ Coupon information – identifies the coupon rate and the type

■ Maturity information – identifies the date at which the security will expire

■ Principal – provides details on the original principal raised by the security

■ Underwriting – information relating the original sale of the security to the market

■ Features – high-level identification of basic features of the bond.

It is worth noting here that terms & conditions data is very closely related to the security descriptive data described earlier. As a general rule of thumb, only information specific to the fixed income asset class appears in this subtype. However, many of these instruments include features that are supported in the security descriptive data subtype – good examples are convertible bonds and ratings. By classifying the content separately in this manner, the global logical data structure supports the specific asset class. This approach goes a long way towards dealing with the complexity inherent in fixed income instruments.

## Redemption information

Bonds and other fixed income instruments can typically be redeemed in one of two circumstances:

■ Maturity – at the instrument's maturity, the principal borrowed by the issuer must be repaid to the holders

■ Event-based – the issuer (and sometimes the holder) has the right, as part of the terms of the security, to force a redemption at a (usually) predetermined time. When invoked by the issuer, the event is referred to as a 'call'; when by the holder, a 'put' (a much less common occurrence).

Redemption information provides a good example of the use of the terms, events and details logic introduced earlier. The two types of redemption are segregated based on the entities – ordinary maturity terms are recorded separately from the call terms and put terms entities. In turn, the event-based redemptions share pretty much the same universe of attributes, reflecting the fact that both describe an event-based redemption.

By and large, all vendor-supplied services provide redemption information in varying degrees of detail. By viewing this content through this logical structure, it provides an easy means to identify when an announcement will impact on the value of a security.

## Floating rate notes

Amongst one of the more complex features a fixed income security may have is the ability to reset its coupon rate in response to other changes in the capital markets. Floating Rate Notes (FRNs) explicitly have such features built into their associated terms. Consequently, this offers investors the ability to ensure that the yield they receive is adjusted in association with other changes, such as a change in interest rates. Equally, they allow holders to minimize the cost of borrowing by setting the coupon rate as a function of some other criterion (such as a central bank rate).

From the data perspective, though, such features are relatively complex to represent. Indeed, the information sources that publish this information do so in very different manners, ranging from full textual descriptions through rather complex use of fields and logic. Quite possibly, FRNs represent some of the most difficult logic associated with capital markets data.

Here again, the standard recurring logic of terms, events and details is used. One key difference introduced here is an extension to the FRN terms entity to include details on the reset formula(e) that can be associated with any one instrument. Identifying the formula type in this manner and recording the associated formula allows for the storage of any formula in the database without imposing a specific structure associated with the formula. In this way, business applications can apply the appropriate logic to the formula as required.

More importantly, this extension illustrates the benefit of using a logical framework to classify and inventory market data content. As any data practitioner can tell you, FRNs are particularly difficult instruments to manage, as by their very nature the projected rate of return changes over time. By looking at these complex instruments through the lens of the logical data framework, these nuances can be made to make a lot more sense.

## Sinking funds

A sinking fund attached to a fixed income instrument affects the ability of the issuer to repay the principal at maturity or other redemption event. Typically, sinking funds, whether whole or part, represent added security to the principal, viewed as reducing risk to the investor.

Within the logical framework, sinking fund information is relatively easy to handle. Most data sources deliver details on the structure of the sinking fund (as terms) and then associated events, almost always on a predetermined schedule. Details associated with any particular event are relatively rare, as the terms typically leave little latitude for flexibility.

## Municipal bonds

An important concept introduced early on was that market data is a function of the intersection of asset classes and data types. An interesting characteristic of this relationship is that as instruments become more specialized, they define their own universe of attributes. From the point of view of a user of market data content, this can prove quite difficult.

Municipal bonds fall into this category. While strictly a bond subtype, their importance, in data content terms, is highlighted by the fact that collectively they represent an enormous stock of investment. This content is primarily sourced from the United States, where these bonds have very special features, typically including tax-exempt status for residents within the state in which the bond is issued. These bonds are also usually (although not always) insured, making them low risk and therefore attractive for many investment portfolios.

Some of the more specialized attributes associated with municipal bond data are:

- Issuance details
- Offering details
- Credit and credit enhancement information
- Escrow details
- Insurance information.

By and large, this information is well handled by the standard terms, events and details logic. Viewed in this manner, the specialized nature of these instruments is reduced to a series of simple extensions within a particular bond subtype.

## Structured products

In like manner to municipal bonds, this fixed income subcategory presents the interesting scenario of the asset class defining the universe of data content, as opposed to the other way round. Referred to collectively as structured products, this subtype groups the information related to three separate bond subtypes:

1. Collateralized mortgage obligations (CMOs)
2. Mortgage backed securities bonds (MBS)
3. Asset backed securities (ABS).

These three bond types all share a common characteristic; they represent a repackaging of other debt (which produces an income stream to the lender). Their chief difference is the quality of the underlying cash flows and how they are packaged into bonds for onwards sale to investors (a process referred to as 'securitization', one of the most complex topics in today's capital markets).

From the point of view of the logical structure of the framework, there are two key characteristics to note:

1. Each of the instrument subtypes has its own child entity
2. All the entities have a relationship to the underlying collateral. Details on collateral, including factors and rates of repayment, are very important for these instruments, as they affect the rate at which the principal is repaid over time.

All other aspects of the bond are captured by the other terms and conditions subtypes.

From the data perspective, structured products is a very specialized content set, made available from only a handful of vendors. As a result, the depth of content available from any one source is inconsistent, making it very difficult to make comparisons.

## PAYMENT INFORMATION

Many securities – not just fixed income instruments – carry associated payment streams. This feature is what makes them of interest to many investors in the first place.

One of the most important criteria in assessing many securities instruments is the manner in which payments are to be made. This is a fundamental characteristic in the evaluation of the instrument and affects a number of factors, including exposure to taxation and cash flow to a portfolio.

Payment information covers a wide variety of factors, including:

- Schedules for when payments will be made
- Rules for accruing interest in the event of missed payments
- Historical records of when payments occurred
- The terms related to details when payments are made on an infrequent basis or payment is made in substitute form (payment in kind).

Taken together, these factors fit the common logic of terms, events and related details as illustrated by Figure 4.12.

## COLLECTIVE INVESTMENTS

Many investments, such as mutual funds and unit trusts, are collections of securities compiled into new instruments. In turn, these securities receive the payment stream (if any) from its constituents, affecting the overall yield.

Within the logical structure of this guide, these sorts of relationships are native. Referred to as collective investments, this data subtype provides a means of capturing the information that is unique to the instruments within this asset class.

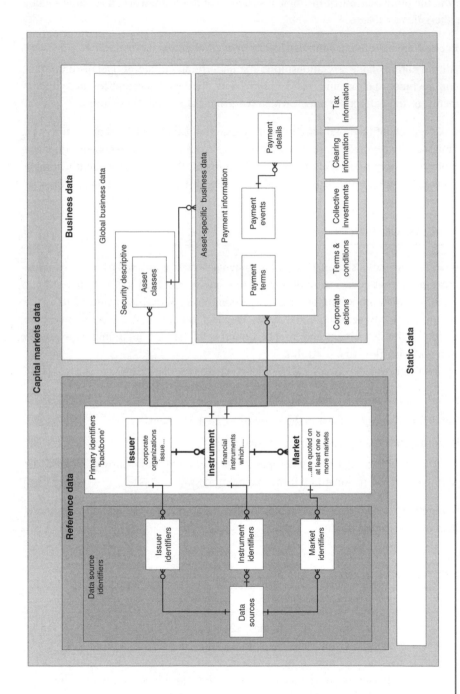

**Figure 4.12** Payment information.

By definition, collective investments are made up of underlying constituents. There-fore, the global relations & constituents data type is used to capture this information. The collective investments subtype captures the remaining information that is pub-lished. These fall into four categories:

1. *Management* – information related to how the fund is managed, including details identifying the portfolio manager and his or her background and style
2. *Holdings* – time-based records for the constituents making up the holdings of the fund or other collective investment vehicle
3. *Performance* – historical records on rates of return and other performance metrics of the fund in comparison with absolute and market benchmarks
4. *Risk measures* – statistical values reflecting the risk profile associated with a par-ticular fund.

Conceptually, the group relates to the funds asset class, as illustrated in Figure 4.13. Each of the four categories is defined in the following subsections.

## Management

A fundamental criterion for evaluating one fund over another is the actual manager (both the firm and the individual). Typically, funds with investment managers that have a good track record find it much easier to raise capital from depositors.

The management subtype groups together the following entities:

■ *Fund details* – providing basic background information about the fund
■ *Investment criteria* – the general strategy or philosophy the manager follows
■ *Fund managers* – historical details on the actual asset manager responsible for the fund, including background on tenure, education and certifications.

Taken together, these address the complete dimension of the quality and track record of the management of the fund.

## Holdings

The strategy and objectives of any collective investment are manifested by what is actu-ally held. There are two elements to the holdings:

1. *Constituents* – the actual holdings at any given time of the fund or other invest-ment vehicle (identified by the relations/constituents data type)
2. *Sector breakdowns* – the allocation of investment within the portfolio to specific sectors, asset classes and geographies.

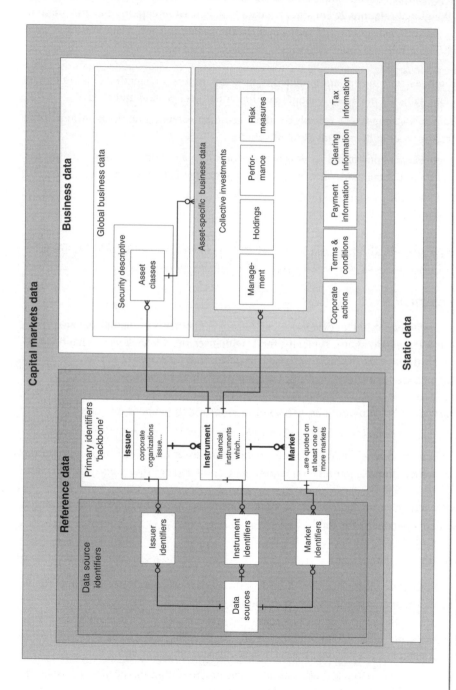

**Figure 4.13** Collective investments.

As the constituents and weightings are handled by the relations/constituents data type described earlier, the holdings subtype needs to deal with only the latter. The subtype breaks the characteristics down into two categories:

1. *Portfolio details* – containing the top level information associated with the holding
2. *Breakdowns* – the definition of the holdings by various criteria, including:
   - country and region allocation
   - asset class and subclass
   - investment style
   - benchmark comparisons

## Performance

All investors seek to find the best possible performance for the lowest acceptable risk. This group of subtypes provides historical measures of the assessment of a fund's performance as judged by independent agencies (such as Morningstar) and market-derived statistics.

Support for performance measures is relatively similar to the means by which ratings are handled for securities. For the period over which the performance assessment applies, a combined value/type combination provides the means of capturing the information. Any future additions and sources for the content are thereby considered as part of the general framework.

## Risk measures

The risk to which a fund or other collective investment vehicle is exposed is a fundamental criterion for investors. Indeed, the risk profile that a fund represents is an important consideration before contributing any monies. As such, many fund managers' investment products are constructed around risk profiles.

As for any financial instrument, there are numerous risk measures used across the industry. As part of the logical framework, these measures that apply to the fund as a whole are maintained as part of this subtype. For the individual constituents of any collective investment, these and other measures are located as part of the trading data type, reflecting the fact that these measures are a product of actual transactions in the market.

## CLEARING INFORMATION

All securities transacted between counterparties need to execute the clearing function. Clearing provides the legal basis under which a transaction is confirmed to have taken place between the counterparties, serving as the basis upon which securities and cash (or equivalent) are exchanged and the trade thereby settled.

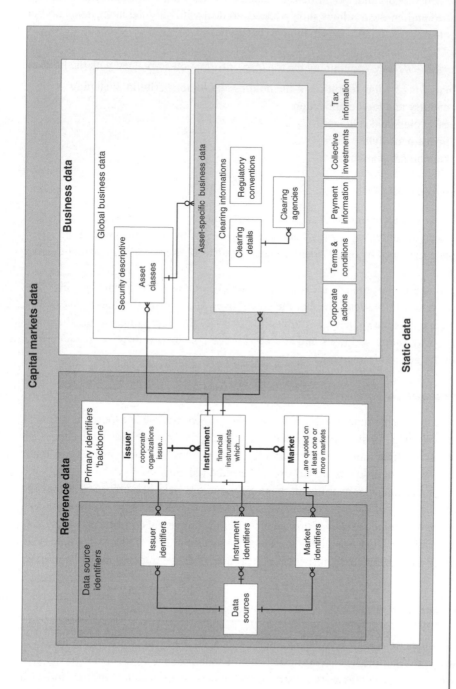

**Figure 4.14** Clearing information.

Clearing occurs in a number of different ways, depending on the asset type. The most common method is for counterparties to outsource clearing to independent third-party clearing agencies – such as the Depository Trust Clearing Corporation (DTCC) in the United Stated, Euroclear in Europe, and the Canadian Depository for Securities in Canada.

There is significant diversity in the regulatory and other requirements associated with clearing. These differences come through, of course, in the nature of the clearing data that is published. It's safe to say, that in today's capital markets, the different clearing regulations and requirements (e.g. 'T+1', 'T+3') all vary based on regulatory regime and, in many cases, asset types.

As such, when it comes to structuring this information a hierarchical representation based around geography is quite useful, as illustrated by Figure 4.14.

As illustrated, the gateway to the clearing data type is via the clearing details entity. The most important function of this relationship is to identify the clearing agency for which deeper information is available. In this way, all details of this highly specialized information set are maintained in one location for each source.

Clearing data remains a relatively specialized subset of the capital markets universe. Elements of the content appear on vendor data services, but by and large there are only a few sources for this information. The irony, of course, is that having defined rules for clearing is fundamental to effective processing of transactions within the industry. Ideally, then, clearing information would form part of all capital markets data applications, allowing for immediate access relevant to each transaction a firm undertakes.

The framework presented here illustrates how, at a logical level, this information can be represented to achieve this goal. Equally, the modular nature of the framework allows for this sort of an incremental approach to representing the content. With the logical structure defined, individual sets of content (based on geography or regulatory regime in this case) can be added as required.

## TAX INFORMATION

Of significant importance to all investors, whether institutional or retail, is the tax treatment of gains and losses incurred from making purchases and sales of securities. No matter the nominal rate of return achieved from financial transactions, the real rate of return to the investor is affected by any taxes payable on the proceeds. Indeed, tax treatment is an important competitive factor between countries seeking investment inflows and capital retention (for future taxation purposes).

Conceptually, the rules associated with tax treatment for individual securities are relatively straightforward, as illustrated in Figure 4.15.

Experience in working with this data shows that the reality is quite different from the concept. It is highly specialized content, and relatively distinctive between sources.

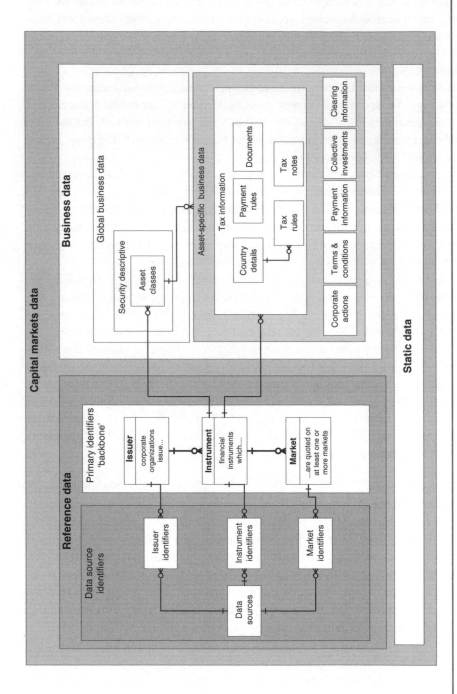

**Figure 4.15** Tax information.

This complexity is not unexpected, given the dependency taxation has on the regulatory regime. This dimension of tax information is further complicated by the fact that within any given country there can also be multiple levels, such as states and provinces. All told, it can quite quickly become very complicated to ascertain the net profit attributable to an investor.

Complexities aside, tax information is increasingly appearing in the industry, both as services from specialist data vendors as well as part of larger, aggregated feeds. This development is the result of increased demand from institutional investors and custodians, primarily as part of their analysis and management activities.

Figure 4.15 is structured around three main components:

1. *Geography* – capturing the relationship to countries, groups of countries (such as the European Union) and constituent states or provinces

2. *Tax type* – taxes typically fall into two categories; income related and capital gains

3. *Notes* – textual descriptions that help to further qualify specific tax rules.

This classification typically catches the tax information that is published in the industry today. In some cases, this approach manages to capture information to the level of individual forms that are required to be completed in order to report to the regulatory authorities.

Ultimately, the ability to capture complete details related to taxation is very difficult. As a result, the tax information services that are available in the capital markets data industry today do not typically provide complete details on every possible transaction. For the moment, the world appears to be quite safe for tax accountants.

# Chapter 5

# Static data

It's pretty fitting that the subject of static data is left to last. The nasty secret of the information industry is that this class of content is almost always thought of after the fact.

Also known as 'domain data' or 'lookup data', this class of market data provides definitions to code values used on all datafeed services. Coded values are routinely used in order to minimize space and support processing efficiency. As a result, for any given code value there needs to be a corresponding definition held elsewhere in what is commonly referred to as a 'lookup table'.

As is common across the market data domain, there are few common standards applied to the content. As a result, there is startling diversity in the coding schemes and definitions used. When it comes to integrating this content into end applications, there is a built in dependency on using the static data from the source. While not overly complex, this can prove problematic.

The real problem comes when applications need to consolidate data content across multiple sources. As each data source produces its own set of code values and definitions, there is little, if any, concordance that can be achieved. The problem is made even worse by the fact that most data sources apply little, if any, quality control to the definitions and their usage. As a result, it is not uncommon to encounter meaningless abbreviations, grammatical mistakes and erroneous or duplicated definitions. These are all common frustrations encountered all too frequently by users of the data content.

Static data falls into two categories:

1. *Global static data* – this provides industry-accepted definitions and coding values. Many data sources carry these standard values in addition to their own proprietary representations

2. *Data type-specific* – values used only within a single data type. These vary considerably between data sources, all of which represent data content in a different format, thereby further increasing the complexity.

The biggest issue to note with static data is the scale. From the point of view of the logical framework introduced here, there are easily over 300 attributes that commonly require static data support. For this collection, the total list of values well exceeds 10 000. Attempting to cross-reference this universe of content across multiple data sources rapidly becomes a very frustrating exercise with little chance of success.

## Global static data

This subset of static data provides definitions that are commonly used by a variety of data type. These coding schemes are produced by recognized sources. The following are well recognized and in common use across the industry:

- Currency codes – three-character ISO standard currency code values and their associated textual definition

- Country codes – both two- and three-character ISO standard country codes are typically used

- Market & exchange codes – a common international standard called the Marketing Identification Code (MIC) has recently become available and is seeing increasing usage

- Industry classifications – over and above vendor classification schemes, there are a number in use, including (among others) the Standard Industrial Classification (SIC) and Morgan Stanley Capital International (MSCI)

■ Security classifications – as with a number of other areas, the ISO has created a standard called Classification for Financial Instruments (CFI). In addition, there are a number of other classification schemes used across the industry, including those produced by financial firms themselves.

As the above list shows, the universe of static data that is supported by accepted standards is relatively small.

## Data type-specific

The second category of static data is, to put it politely, very diverse. Different data services deliver data content in different ways. Where one feed uses a code value and associated static data, another provides the definition as part of the content. There are no rules and, worse, no quality standards.

To market data users, this presents a major challenge. All too frequently, the support for static data is assumed to be in line with the other content provided by the data source.

# Chapter 6

# Logical data dictionary

This chapter lays out a series of attributes associated with each of the data types given in the logical framework, along with an associated definition, relevant for users of this guide. It should be noted that this is intended to provide basic, logical definition understanding for use within the framework provided by this guide. More detailed definitions, of course, should be provided as part of any implementation.

The dictionary follows the logical framework used throughout the guide. All content is grouped by the combination of data class, data subclass, data type and data subtype defined in detail in the body of the guide. The objective is to put forward the most commonly encountered attributes from vendor datafeed services and other data sources.

Taken as a whole, then, this collection of terms provides the logical data dictionary associated with the general framework. The aim is to provide these details in order to qualify fully the contents of the hierarchy introduced by this guide – if a picture speaks a thousand words, then examples are equally useful when discussing capital markets data.

These objectives should be clearly noted. This dictionary is not intended to define any single physical implementation or data source. Rather, it provides a general guideline to better understanding the content produced by the global capital markets.

## Market data class: reference data

Reference data is defined as the universe of attributes that describe an issuer, a financial instrument or a market quote, and their associated interrelationships.

### DATA TYPE: BACKBONE

This subclass is made up of attributes that identify an issuer, instrument or market item uniquely within the framework.

### Data subtype: issuer

The issuer subtype contains information that describes and defines the organization that issues financial instruments. By definition, issuer information is global in nature, as it sits atop the logical hierarchy of issuer to instrument to market.

| Attribute | Definition |
|---|---|
| Issuer identifier | An alphanumeric string that uniquely identifies issuer organizations. Within the capital markets industry, there is no single standard issuer identifier that is wholly adopted. As such, many data vendors create and issue their own proprietary schemes. Consequently, much of the task of identification is based on using issuer names and industrial classifications. |
| Headquarters location | Where an issuer's headquarters is located is typically used in identifying issuers uniquely. Usually expressed as a country code – the two- and three-character ISO standards are commonly carried by most data vendor services. |

| Attribute | Definition |
|---|---|
| Primary name | All issuers have a primary name by which they are recognized. They may also have one or more alternate names, which can lead to extensive duplication in applications. |
| Corporate status | A flag to indicate if a company actually is in business and active. Companies that have ceased trading can still be important for many applications, and as a result need to be considered within the scope. |
| Data source | The source used to populate information that defines a specific issuer is very important. As multiple sources likely carry information on many of the same issuers, it is a defining element in unique identification. |

## Data subtype: instrument

The instrument subtype contains information that describes and defines individual financial securities. Within the capital markets data universe this is fundamental and required by almost all applications, as it identifies specifically the instrument transacted between two counterparties, regardless of the market in which the transaction takes place.

| Attribute | Definition |
|---|---|
| Instrument identifier | An alphanumeric string used to identify securities. There are many different schemes in use to identify securities as well as international standards such as ISIN. As a result, cross-referencing between the various coding schemes is a fundamental requirement for working with market data. |
| Asset classification | A fundamental attribute to identifying any instrument is the asset class to which it belongs. Regardless of the scheme used, the assignment of the instrument to a particular asset class is essential in order to access the supporting business data content. |
| Data source | The source used to populate information that defines a specific instrument is very important. As multiple sources always carry information on many of the same securities, it is a defining element in unique identification. |

*(Continued)*

| Attribute | Definition |
|---|---|
| Security name | The common name used to identify instruments. A variety of conventions are used by sources for market data. Not as widely used as the issuer primary name. |
| Currency | All securities are denominated in a currency of issue. Usually expressed as a country code – the two- and three-character ISO standards are commonly carried by most data vendor services. |
| Security status | A flag to indicate whether a security is considered active or not. Securities can change their status for many reasons (called, matured, etc.) and so it is fundamental to unique identification as many applications implicitly require only active securities data content. |
| Issue date | The date an instrument was formally issued to the market for trading. |

## Data subtype: market

The market data subtype is at the lowest level of the logical hierarchy and provides the most detailed information related to an instrument. No security can be transacted without this information, since it defines fundamental characteristics of a transaction such as the currency in which the deal takes place and the relevant conventions. Since the hierarchical relationship of the backbone is one to many, market-level information typically represents by far the largest number of records.

| Attribute | Definition |
|---|---|
| Market identifier | An alphanumeric string used to identify securities on a particular market. There are many different schemes in use to identify securities as well as international standards such as SEDOL. As a result, cross-referencing between the various coding schemes is a fundamental requirement for working with market data. |
| Market | Usually a coded value, used to indicate the market on which an instrument trades. Markets include regulated |

| Attribute | Definition |
| --- | --- |
| | entities such as exchanges, as well as over-the-counter locations such as cities (e.g. London for LIBOR rates). |
| Market name | A textual name supplied by the data vendor associated with the instrument at the market level. |
| Currency | The currency in which the security trades in the associated market. Usually expressed as a country code – the two- and three-character ISO standards are commonly carried by most data vendor services. |
| Unit of quotation | Identifies the currency and the units in which the instrument is quoted on a particular exchange or, possibly, over the counter (e.g. USD/Barrel or GBP/ Kilo etc.). |
| Market issue date | The date on which the security was added to the particular market (typically a securities exchange). |
| Market rules and conventions | All markets have regulations governing transactions between counterparties and their subsequent confirmation and exchange. This information is by definition related to individual markets such as exchanges. |

## DATA TYPE: DATA SOURCE INFORMATION

This reference data subclass is made up of identifiers and related information as provided by the source for the data content. Linking the source for data content with the actual values is an extremely important (although typically implied) component to market data, as the same attribute may (and often does) contain different values from different sources, depending on a number of factors. Indeed, with increased regulatory compliance increasingly coming into effect in the global capital markets, maintaining the attribution to the data content is becoming a mandatory requirement for many business functions within financial firms.

## Data subtype: identifiers

The identifiers subtype groups together the many various identification schemes used in the industry. There is a wide variety of schemes used at all three of the issuer, instrument, and market levels of the hierarchy. Since different data sources can all make use of the same universe of identifiers (plus their own proprietary in-house schemes), they can be viewed as sharing the same subtype.

| Attribute | Definition |
|---|---|
| Identifier | One of an issuer, an instrument or a market identifier to provide the link between the core reference data and these cross-references. |
| Identifier code value | The actual value (usually an alphanumeric string) used to identify issuers, instruments or market entities uniquely. Values must be used in conjunction with the code type definition (i.e. name/value pair) in order to be meaningful. |
| Identifier code type | Identifies the type of code scheme used to identify issuers, instruments and market items uniquely. A wide variety of identifiers are used across the industry, with no one definitive standard in use globally. |

### Data subtype: sources

The sources subtype groups together identification of the origin of particular data content. As the same source can be associated with identifiers at all three levels of the hierarchy, these can naturally be grouped into a single location for easy reference.

| Attribute | Definition |
|---|---|
| Identifier | One of an issuer, an instrument or a market identifier to provide the link between the core reference data and the source used to populate the reference and business data. |
| Identifier code type | Identifies the type of code scheme used to identify issuers, instruments and market items uniquely. A wide variety of identifiers are used across the industry, with no one definitive standard in use globally. |
| Data source | An alphanumeric string that identifies the source for the content used to populate reference and business data attributes. With a very wide and diverse population of data sources in the industry covering a variety of asset class and data types, identification is essential in ensuring consistency and accuracy. |

# ■ Market data class: business data

This class of market data refers to the universe of attributes that describe a particular aspect of an issuer, instrument or market entity as it pertains to specific business data applications. Business data represents easily the largest universe of attributes within this logical framework.

## DATA TYPE: GLOBAL

The global business data type refers to those entities and attributes that apply to all instrument types or asset classes.

### Data subtype: security descriptive data

The security descriptive global business data subtype provides the basic descriptive information related to financial instruments.

#### Security details
Security details contain attributes that describe and define a particular financial instrument. Often such details are used to confirm that counterparties refer to the same instrument, as identifiers can sometimes not agree.

| Attribute | Definition |
|---|---|
| Instrument identifier | An alphanumeric string used to identify securities. There are many different schemes in use to identify securities as well as international standards such as ISIN. As a result, cross-referencing between the various coding schemes is a fundamental requirement for working with market data. |
| Issue date | The calendar date on which the instrument was made available to the financial markets. |
| Instrument name | The textual name of the instrument. Conventions are used by data sources and issuers in defining the names associated with the instrument. |
| Prospectus identifier | A coded value that serves to cross-reference the financial instrument with its associated investment contract or prospectus. The prospectus provides full legal definition of the financial instrument. |
| Instrument type | A coded value that identifies the kind of instrument. A wide variety of methods and classifications is used by sources of market data. |

## Asset classes

The asset class identifies the category to which a financial instrument is classified. In turn, this classification determines the list of attributes that define the instrument. The logical framework described here is based on a relatively simple classification scheme representing the most commonly encountered instrument types in today's capital markets.

| Attribute | Definition |
|---|---|
| Instrument identifier | An alphanumeric string used to identify securities. There are many different schemes in use to identify securities as well as international standards such as ISIN. As a result, cross-referencing between the various coding schemes is a fundamental requirement for working with market data. |
| Debt/fixed income | Securities that represent borrowing by the issuer. By definition, all fixed income securities have an associated maturity date and rate of payment. |
| Equity | A financial instrument representing a share in the ownership of the issuing organization. |
| Money market | Financial instruments usually issued with a maturity date of less than 1 year. In addition, this asset class also includes spot and forward currency rates. |
| Derivatives | Financial instruments that derive their value from other underlying instruments. Examples include options, futures and swap contracts. |
| Collective investments | The term used to define instruments such as mutual funds and unit investment trusts that are made up of one or more underlying constituents. These instruments differ from derivatives, as they represent actual ownership of the constituent securities in the portfolio. |
| Indices | Statistical measures of the performance of a given group of financial instruments such as a market. Indices are widely used to serve as a benchmark and as the underlying factor in derivative contracts. |

## Security features

A financial instrument may have one or more specific features that can be invoked by either the issuer or the holder. The nature of these features (for example, convertibility into another security) greatly affects the attractiveness of the security to investors.

| Attribute | Definition |
|---|---|
| Instrument identifier | An alphanumeric string used to identify securities. There are many different schemes in use to identify securities as well as international standards such as ISIN. As a result, cross-referencing between the various coding schemes is a fundamental requirement for working with market data. |
| Feature type | A coded value that identifies the particular feature associated with the instrument. A given security can have many features, depending on its asset classification and complexity, as defined by its underlying prospectus or other investment contract. |
| Feature description | Financial instruments can have a number of specific associated features, depending on the terms defined in the underlying investment contract. Most data sources provide a variety of features in the form of coded values, requiring cross-referencing to their associated definitions provided as accompany static data. By definition, features vary by asset class and sometimes by the market in which the instrument is traded. |

## Security classification schemes

Where asset classes are used in the framework to provide a high-level navigation between the various instrument types, security classification schemes provide very detailed categorization. As there are a number of different schemes used by the industry, including proprietary schemes from individual data sources, this is a relatively complex data type – further complicated by the lack of concordance between the various schemes.

| Attribute | Definition |
|---|---|
| Instrument identifier | An alphanumeric string used to identify securities. There are many different schemes in use to identify securities as well as international standards such as ISIN. As a result, cross-referencing between the various coding schemes is a fundamental requirement for working with market data. |

*(Continued)*

| Attribute | Definition |
|---|---|
| Security classification scheme | Multiple security classification schemes are used in the industry (e.g. ISO CFI) with little or no mutual concordance. In addition, any one data source carrying instrument data is likely to offer multiple coding schemes in order to support customers. Therefore, this attribute is essential to specify, in order to allocate the security to a particular category – a common requirement for many investment criteria and analysis. |
| Security classification value | Usually an alphanumeric value defined by a particular schema. Both text and numeric values are used. |
| Classification date | Within a given classification scheme, instrument can have their classification modified. By keeping a record of dates on which these changes are made, a full historical record is created. |

### Third parties

Contains information on service providers associated with all three of the issuer, instrument and market levels of the logical hierarchy. A complete list of relevant third parties is very important for supporting efficient administration of securities and trading activities.

| Attribute | Definition |
|---|---|
| Instrument identifier | An alphanumeric string used to identify securities. There are many different schemes in use to identify securities as well as international standards such as ISIN. As a result, cross-referencing between the various coding schemes is a fundamental requirement for working with market data. |
| Third-party type | An indication of the role the third party plays (e.g. transfer agent, custodian, etc.) |
| Third-party name | The trade name of the third-party organization – ideally, the same name used as the corporate primary name. |

### Conversion terms

This provides details on the means by which one security can be converted into one or more other securities. These are complex transactions with numerous qualifying criteria.

| Attribute | Definition |
| --- | --- |
| Instrument identifier | An alphanumeric string used to identify securities. There are many different schemes in use to identify securities as well as international standards such as ISIN. As a result, cross-referencing between the various coding schemes is a fundamental requirement for working with market data. |
| Conversion terms | Details originally sourced from the prospectus that lay out the conditions under which a security can be converted into another. Such transactions are relatively complex and time-sensitive. Specific attributes to consider include schedule and period, conversion price, conversion security, amount of an issue that can be converted, the associated currency, notification requirements, etc. |
| Conversion events | A historical record of the conversion of one security into another including the instrument identifier, the target identifier (if any), start date, end date, etc. |
| Conversion details | Additional details related to individual conversion events. Many conversion terms allow for flexibility in setting the details for a specific event (such as the price), and therefore can vary by event. |

## *Data subtype: trading data*

This subtype contains details (such as price) that refer to the exchange of financial instruments between counterparties. It easily represents the most commonly encountered and most voluminous subset of market data.

### Pricing data

Pricing data is made up of attributes that describe the economic value and liquidity of a financial instrument in a given market at a given time. It is widely used across the industry.

| Attribute | Definition |
|-----------|-----------|
| Market identifier | An alphanumeric string used to identify securities on a particular market. There are many different schemes in use to identify securities as well as international standards such as SEDOL. As a result, cross-referencing between the various coding schemes is a fundamental requirement for working with market data. |
| Pricing fact | A wide number of trading facts are used across the industry. Most commonly used are open, high, low, close, volume, bid, and ask prices. In order to be meaningful, price values must always be associated with a particular pricing fact. |
| Pricing value | The actual value associated with a price fact. |
| Pricing date | The date associated with a pricing value and price fact combination. The date is a fundamental attribute in making the price value relevant for business applications. |
| Pricing time | The time during a given day at which the price value was recorded. This is a fundamental requirement for realtime data, as price quotes are differentiated by the time at which they are made. |
| Sequence number | An optional attribute that is quite useful and commonly used is a number that records the order in which the updates for a particular pricing value are received. Used in ordering the pricing values, this also helps to qualify the liquidity associated with an instrument, as a higher number of updates is typically associated with securities that can trade easily. |
| Price type | An important characteristic for many instruments is the price type that is quoted by the market (for example, with or without interest, ex or cum dividend). Such details affect the actual cash flow to the holder of the security, hence this is an important attribute to define. |
| Price source | Primarily associated with over-the-counter trading, knowing the actual price source for a quote can be particularly important. A broad number of price sources indicates a more liquid market for the instrument. Equally, it can help to better qualify the actual price values being quoted – if the price source is a declared market maker, the price is quoted to fulfill regulatory commitments and not necessarily the best indication of the market's valuation of the instrument (although the reverse can also be true). |

## Aggregated and derived data

This data consists of statistical values that are based on and/or calculated from underlying pricing data attributes. The industry uses a wide range of statistical values, depending on the nature of the asset and the type of analysis.

| Attribute | Definition |
|---|---|
| Market identifier | An alphanumeric string used to identify securities on a particular market. There are many different schemes in use to identify securities as well as international standards such as SEDOL. As a result, cross-referencing between the various coding schemes is a fundamental requirement for working with market data. |
| Statistic type | The use of derived statistics is very common across the financial industry. Naturally, these values are carried as part of vendor data services. As these values are not directly quoted by the market, they fall into a separate category within the trading data subtype. Examples of such derived statistical values include Price–Earnings Ratio, Volatility. Aggregate values include total market volume, total number of advancing/declining price values etc. There is no defined list of these statistics in use across the industry. Indeed, proprietary statistical calculation is an important competitive differentiator between firms. |
| Statistic value | The calculated value associated with the statistic type. As with pricing, this is a fundamental requirement for using the statistical values. |
| Pricing date | The date associated with a statistic value, statistic type combination. The date is a fundamental attribute in making the value relevant for business applications and analysis. |
| Pricing time | The time during a given day at which the value was recorded. |
| Sequence number | An optional attribute that is quite useful and commonly used is a number that records the order in which the updates for a particular value are received. Used in ordering the values chronologically, this also helps to qualify the liquidity associated with an instrument, as a higher number of updates is typically associated with securities that can trade easily. |

### Trading notes

Trading financial instruments is a complex business, especially in the over-the-counter markets. As such, keeping additional textual notes can be extraordinarily important for a variety of reasons, including compliance and post-trade processing.

| Attribute | Definition |
|---|---|
| Market identifier | An alphanumeric string used to identify securities on a particular market. There are many different schemes in use to identify securities as well as international standards such as SEDOL. As a result, cross-referencing between the various coding schemes is a fundamental requirement for working with market data. |
| Trade date | The date for which the note applies. |
| Trade time | The time during a given day at which the note was recorded. Usually trade notes apply on a daily basis, although a timestamp is always useful. |
| Note | During any given trading day it is not uncommon for notices to be issued that provide additional explanatory or regulatory information. These notes appear in a variety of forms on vendor services, and to a greater and lesser extent. Notes are very useful for identifying relevant events such as trade suspension, delisting announcements and other explanatory information useful to market participants. |

## Data subtype: issuer & corporate data

The issuer & corporate data subtype groups together descriptive information related to issuers.

### Issuer information

This provides basic descriptive information to identify and described fully the issuer organization. This information provides the basic descriptive criteria used in evaluating the performance and other aspect of companies and other issuers.

| Attribute | Definition |
|---|---|
| Issuer identifier | An alphanumeric value (usually a number) that identifies issuers, such as corporations, uniquely. Data sources typically publish their own proprietary values, |

| Attribute | Definition |
|-----------|------------|
| | although there are some independent conventions available (CUSIP 6 is an example). Typically, all issuer-level business data is linked using the issuer identifier. |
| Alternate name(s) | One of the more frustrating aspects of working with issuer-level data content is the use of multiple names and abbreviations associated with any one issuer. Most data services provide at least one alternate name by which the issuer is recognized in the industry, and sometimes several. Unfortunately there is little consistency across the various sources in the industry, leading to significant challenges for applications such as searching, which tend to return duplicates, limiting effectiveness. |
| Country information | At the issuer level, country information is relevant in variety of areas. In the case of government issuers, it is a fundamental attribute. Typical country-level information that is relevant to capital markets data includes country of headquarters, country of listing, country of registration and country of issue. |
| Addresses | Closely linked to country information. Almost all financial contracts require issuers to list their physical location as part of the prospectus or other legal documentation. As issuers can have multiple locations along with their subsidiaries who may also issue securities, an up-to-date physical address can be very important for a variety of administrative functions – such as remitting payments. |
| Key personnel | Closely followed by investors and analysts are the key executive personnel. Changes to positions such as the CEO and CFO can easily lead to major price swings of a corporation's securities. |
| Press releases | A commonly used marketing and notification channel is press releases. These pre-formatted statements are used to announce events which can lead to changes in securities prices. |
| News stories | Many data sources offer news services in addition to capital markets data. Indeed, for a number of applications, such as trading, the two cannot be separated. While not usually considered strictly within the scope of capital markets data, this close relationship makes the two very tightly coupled. |

## Performance data

Common to all business organizations is accounting information reported on a regular basis. Made up of such common items as balance sheets, income statements, cash flow statements and other measures, performance data is widely used by the financial markets as a means of assessing the success (or failure) of issuer organizations.

| Attribute | Definition |
|---|---|
| Issuer identifier | An alphanumeric value (usually a number) that identifies issuers, such as corporations, uniquely. Data sources typically publish their own proprietary values, although there are some independent conventions available (CUSIP 6 is an example). Typically all issuer level business data is linked using the issuer identifier. |
| Reporting period | A statement of the period for which performance data is reported is an essential attribute. The timeframe for which the measures apply (typically quarterly or annual) is mandatory in order to apply the data content. |
| Reporting frequency | Publicly listed companies are required to report financial results on a regular basis. This attribute is therefore fundamental in the use of performance data. |
| Balance sheet | A regular statement of a company's assets and liabilities. Balance sheets are closely tracked, as they provide a snapshot of the financial health of an issuer. In particular, significant changes to balance-sheet values can lead to major swings in prices of securities. There is considerable geographic diversity in the make-up of balance sheets. Comparison of balance sheets across countries can be quite difficult, given different accounting standards. A number of data vendor firms aggregate and consolidate this content to support comparison and evaluation. |
| Income statement | A regular statement of the generation and net make-up of revenues. |
| Cash flows | A detailed report on the make-up of revenue generation and expenditure. |
| Forecasts/estimates | Forward-looking estimates of an issuer's performance, forecasts are published by third parties such as analysts as well as by issuers themselves (in order to provide 'guidance' to the industry). Estimates are monitored widely and used as the basis for assessing business |

| Attribute | Definition |
|---|---|
| Financial ratios | performance of the issuer over upcoming reporting periods.<br>Derived statistics from various performance data are widely used by analysts and investors. These values provide an empirical measure of a company's health, and serve the purpose of supporting meaningful comparisons of performance. |

## Industry classifications

In similar fashion to security classification schemes, issuer organizations are categorized based on industry. There are a number of classification schemes in use as well as proprietary data vendor schemes, with little or no concordance between them. Industry classifications are widely used as a means of monitoring performance of issuer organizations within specific sectors and undertaking benchmark comparisons.

| Attribute | Definition |
|---|---|
| Issuer identifier | An alphanumeric value (usually a number) that identifies issuers, such as corporations, uniquely. Data sources typically publish their own proprietary values, although there are some independent conventions available (CUSIP 6 is an example). Typically, all issuer-level business data is linked using the issuer identifier. |
| Classification scheme | Multiple industrial classification schemes are used in the industry (SIC, MSCI, etc.). In addition, any one data source carrying corporate business data is likely to offer multiple coding schemes in order to support customers. Therefore, this attribute is essential to specify in order to allocate the issuer to a business sector – a common requirement for many investment criteria and analysis. |
| Classification value | Usually an alphanumeric value defined by a particular schema. Both text and numeric values are used. |
| Classification date | Within a given classification scheme, issuers can have their classification modified as their business changes due to acquisitions, divestments and so on. By keeping a record of dates on which these changes are made, a full historical record is created. |

## Ownership and holdings

This provides details on the subsidiaries and other holdings one issuer may have in another. Such arm's-length relationships can have a significant impact on the risk profile of purchasing instruments from a given issuer.

| Attribute | Definition |
|---|---|
| Issuer identifier | An alphanumeric value (usually a number) that identifies issuers, such as corporations, uniquely. Data sources typically publish their own proprietary values, although there are some independent conventions available (CUSIP 6 is an example). Typically, all issuer-level business data is linked using the issuer identifier. |
| Ownership interest | An identification of the company or instrument holding of the corporation identified by the issuer identifier in another company. There are a variety of methods of identifying these interests, including the target issuer identifier, instrument identifiers and even company primary and alternate names. |
| Ownership amount | The level of ownership held by the company identified by the issuer identifier in the target company. Typically expressed as a percentage value. |
| Ownership type | Usually a textual description of the interest held – examples include 'wholly subsidiary', 'common share holding %' etc. |

## *Data subtype: ratings*

The ratings subtype applies to both the instrument and issuer levels. Independent agencies monitor and report on the investment-worthiness of companies and the individual securities they issue. Changes in ratings value from high-profile international ratings agencies such as Moody's or Standard & Poor's can lead to a dramatic change in price in securities.

| Attribute | Definition |
|---|---|
| Issuer identifier (for corporate ratings) | An alphanumeric value (usually a number) that identifies issuers, such as corporations, uniquely. Data sources typically publish their own proprietary values, although there are some independent conventions available (CUSIP 6 is an example). Typically, all issuer-level business data is linked using the issuer identifier. |

| Attribute | Definition |
|---|---|
| Instrument identifier (for securities ratings) | An alphanumeric string used to identify securities. There are many different schemes in use to identify securities as well as international standards such as ISIN. As a result, cross-referencing between the various coding schemes is a fundamental requirement for working with market data. |
| Rating agency | Identifies the agency assigning the associated quality rating. Commonly known agencies include Standard & Poor's, Moody's, and Fitch, as well as a number of other firms focusing on specific geographical markets. |
| Rating value | The actual value issued by the rating agency. As each agency has its own proprietary rating scheme, it is essential to maintain the agency and rating type along with the rating value. |
| Rating date | The date on which the most recent rating was changed. Maintaining the date is important, as it allows for historical records to be kept – since ratings changes typically affect securities prices (either positively or negatively), this association is very important. |
| Rating type | Identifies whether the quality rating is the regular (standard) agency rating, a standard equity ranking or an indicator supplemental to the standard rating or ranking. |
| Comments | Like trading notes, additional textual commentary is commonly associated with ratings information. |

## Data subtype: relations/constituents

Used at both the instrument and issuer levels, this subtype captures the relationships between groups and their constituents. A wide variety of relationships is implied within market data content which, when collated, form an independent subtype within the logical framework.

| Attribute | Definition |
|---|---|
| Instrument identifier | An alphanumeric string used to identify securities. There are many different schemes in use to identify securities as well as international standards such as ISIN. As a result, cross-referencing between |

(Continued)

| Attribute | Definition |
|---|---|
| | the various coding schemes is a fundamental requirement for working with market data. |
| Relationship type | A definition of the nature of the relationship that is in effect. Relationships can exist between issuer entities, securities and market entities. Examples include constituents (of, for example, a fund or an index), holdings of subsidiaries and members of an index. |
| Related instrument identifier(s) | Where the relationship type is between securities (for example, a mutual fund is made of constituent instruments), a record of the related identifiers. By associating the underlying instrument identifiers with the instrument identifier, the list of constituents is defined. |
| Weighting(s) | The percentage value the security holds as a constituent in the group of securities identified by the related instrument identifier. |
| Issuer identifier | An alphanumeric value (usually a number) that identifies issuers, such as corporations, uniquely. Data sources typically publish their own proprietary values, although there are some independent conventions available (CUSIP 6 is an example). Typically, all issuer-level business data is linked using the issuer identifier. |
| Related issuer identifiers | Where the relationship type is between corporate entities (for example, a subsidiary), a record of the related identifiers. By associating the underlying issuer identifiers, the list of constituents is defined. |

## DATA TYPE: ASSET-SPECIFIC

Much of the universe of capital markets data is unique to the asset classification of the instrument. As a result, market data contains many detailed and specific attributes that are unique to any one asset type. In addition, this is further complicated by the fact that some subsets of asset-specific data can also apply to other, usually closely related, instrument subtypes. Within the logical framework these attributes are grouped into various subtypes, therefore making up the asset-specific data type.

## *Data subtype: corporate actions*

This refers to the universe of business events that can have a material impact on the value of securities issued by an organization or their holders. Within this logical framework, corporate actions fall into three main categories:

1. Events that represent notification of the exercising of terms associated with an instrument
2. Notification of the terms associated with an instrument failing to be met
3. Events that affect the value of the security at arm's length.

At the highest level, common attributes that identify a corporate action event are as follows.

| Attribute | Definition |
| --- | --- |
| Instrument identifier | An alphanumeric string used to identify securities. There are many different schemes in use to identify securities as well as international standards such as ISIN. As a result, cross-referencing between the various coding schemes is a fundamental requirement for working with market data. |
| Announcement date | The date (and sometimes the time) when notification of the corporate actions event is made. |
| Event identifier | A unique identifier value (usually a number) used to identify the event. Identifiers are important, as they allow for separate events affecting a given security to be recorded. |
| Event type | A categorization of the event. There is considerable diversity in the universe of corporate actions events provided by data vendors and other sources, and no single standard yet exists. This framework sets the initial scope as announcements relating to exercising terms, announcements that terms of a security will not be met, and announcements that affect the security indirectly. |
| Announcement status | The standing of the event at the announcement date. As corporate actions are event-based, their status changes over time. The typical cycle tends to include 'preliminary', 'actual' and 'revised' announcements. The use of the sequence number allows for this cycle to be monitored. |

*(Continued)*

| Attribute | Definition |
|---|---|
| Sequence number | An optional attribute that is quite useful and commonly used is a number that records the order in which the update for a particular corporate action event is announced. This provides an audit trail to support business applications that take action in response to an announcement. |

### Exercising of terms

Likely the most common form of corporate action events is the exercising of terms that are associated with an instrument. For the most part, the impact of these events is relatively easy to predict and qualify in advance. It should be noted that these events typically occur as a series of announcements, each adding more detail and confirming previous information. As such, it is essential to avoid viewing corporate actions as being static – they can and do update, sometimes with dramatic changes, on an incremental basis. Examples of this corporate actions subtype include:

■ Dividends – payment either in cash or in kind of surplus profits to shareholders
■ Capital changes – modifications to the capital structure of the issuing organization. Examples include new issues, rights issues, share splits, dilution events and shares outstanding changes.

Market data attributes typically encountered include the following.

| Attribute | Definition |
|---|---|
| Instrument identifier | An alphanumeric string used to identify securities. There are many different schemes in use to identify securities as well as international standards such as ISIN. As a result, cross-referencing between the various coding schemes is a fundamental requirement for working with market data. |
| Event identifier | A unique identifier value (usually a number) used to identify the event. Identifiers are important, as they allow for separate events affecting a given security to be recorded. |
| Term identifier | The specific type of event within the category. Typical examples include dividend announcements, capital structure changes, etc. |

| Attribute | Definition |
|-----------|------------|
| Date type | Corporate actions have a number of specific date constraints that are declared by the issuer or their third-party agent in line with regulatory requirements. These include the record date, pay date, recision date, and ex-date. Multiple date types typically apply to any one corporate action announcement, and values can be revised over the life of the event. |
| Date value | The actual calendar date value associated with the individual date type. |
| Period | Indicates the length of time on a calendar basis (usually a start and end date combination) over which an event is monitored. Most commonly used with regular events such as dividend declarations. |
| Frequency | The periodicity of the announcement. Many corporate actions events, such as dividend announcement, occur over fixed frequency, while others are entirely event-based, such as a share split. |
| Previous value | The previously announced value of the term. As corporate actions by definition announce changes, having both the previous and new values supports comparison. |
| New value | The announced value of the term. As corporate actions by definition announce changes, having both the previous and new values support comparison. |
| Amount | Where the event involves a payment, the amount declared by the issuer. |
| Currency code | The currency associated with an amount. |
| Units | The unit in which the amount is quoted. This is an important attribute as many corporate actions events are quoted either as a total or on a per instrument (shares in particular) basis. |

### Failure to meet instrument terms

Corporate actions events are highly context-sensitive. Announcements that may have a significant effect on one investor may not be considered particularly important by another. It is this complexity in impact that differentiates corporate actions from the other data types making up the framework. In particular, the failure of an issuer to meet the terms associated with an instrument – such as failing to make a scheduled coupon payment – can have major implications impacting not only the holder but also ongoing valuation of the security.

| Attribute | Definition |
|---|---|
| Instrument identifier | An alphanumeric string used to identify securities. There are many different schemes in use to identify securities as well as international standards such as ISIN. As a result, cross-referencing between the various coding schemes is a fundamental requirement for working with market data. |
| Event identifier | A unique identifier value (usually a number) used to identify the event. Identifiers are important, as they allow for separate events affecting a given security to be recorded. |
| Event description | Textual descriptions of the event and its cause(s) are almost always involved in this corporate actions subtype. |
| Sequence number | Multiple updates providing more information about this class of corporate actions events are almost always certain. Failing to meet terms of an instrument call lead to a lot of dialogue between holders of the instrument and the issuer, resulting in follow-on notifications. As such, a sequence number is essential in order to build and maintain a full audit trail of the event. |
| Attribute identifier(s) | The name of the attribute that is affected by the event. Examples include 'coupon rate', 'payment amount', 'maturity date'. |
| Notification date | The date the notification was made by the issuer or their agents (see 'third parties'). All corporate actions events within this subtype are highly time-sensitive. Therefore, maintaining a record of the dates is essential in order to create and manage an audit trail. |
| Notification type | Depending on the data source, a code value of some form that identifies the nature of the notification. Corporate actions events almost always are delivered as part of a series from the original notice through to further updates that add new information and others that represent corrections. |
| Amount | Common to most corporate actions announcements in this class is the total value affected by the event. |
| Currency | The currency associated with the amount announced as part of the event notification. |

### Indirect/reorganization announcements

Perhaps the most common form of corporate actions events are announcements that affect the instruments issued by an organization in an indirect manner. These announcements are commonly delivered via the press. Some have a direct bearing on the issuing firm, others affect other firms (such as in an acquisition announcement). In common with all corporate actions event types, these announcements are typically delivered as a series and are not static. For example, the act of a merger between two firms will have numerous changes (company name, for example) and require many updates over a significant time period.

| Attribute | Definition |
|---|---|
| Instrument identifier | An alphanumeric string used to identify securities. There are many different schemes in use to identify securities as well as international standards such as ISIN. As a result, cross-referencing between the various coding schemes is a fundamental requirement for working with market data. |
| Event identifier | A unique identifier value (usually a number) used to identify the event. Identifiers are important, as they allow for separate events affecting a given security to be recorded. |
| Reorganization event type | A general category to which the event is assigned. As part of this subtype, there is a considerable diversity encountered on vendor information services. |
| Effective date | The date on which the event will take effect. |
| Event description | A detailed textual description of the event with complete details as appropriate for the nature of the event. |
| Notice type | By their very nature events in this subtype can receive a number of different notifications – examples include preliminary, information only, etc. |
| Sequence number | An optional attribute that is quite helpful and commonly used is a number that records the order in which the update for a particular corporate action event is announced. This provides an audit trail to support business applications that take action in response to an announcement. |

## Data subtype: terms & conditions

Primarily related to instruments traded over the counter, and bonds in particular, the terms and conditions data subtype is possibly one of the most complex sets of capital markets data. All sources of fixed income data content (as well as some others) to a greater or lesser extent publish elements of this information; however, there is no single representation or standard that is widely followed. Consequently, terms & conditions data is highly varied between sources.

As the name implies, this subtype captures the defining characteristics of the instrument and the rules under which they can be exercised. As a result, this data subtype covers a very broad range of highly detailed information grouped into the following categories:

- Summary information
- Redemption information
- Floating rate note details
- Sinking fund information
- Municipal bond details
- Structured products details.

### Summary information

This terms & conditions subtype refers to the collection of data elements that are common across the instruments making up the asset class (typically fixed income). Taken collectively, the attributes making up this subtype provide the basic descriptive information that distinguishes one instrument type (for example, a treasury bond) from another (such as a municipal bond).

| Attribute | Definition |
|---|---|
| Instrument identifier | An alphanumeric string used to identify securities. There are many different schemes in use to identify securities as well as international standards such as ISIN. As a result, cross-referencing between the various coding schemes is a fundamental requirement for working with market data. |
| Bond type | Provided either as part of a security classification schema or by itself, the category of fixed income instruments determine to a large extent the terms associated with the instrument. There are a number of conventions used which go to differing levels of detail. Typical bond types include government, corporate, agency, municipal, etc. |
| Issuance details | Information related to the issuing of the security. Typically, attributes to consider include issue size, price, discount, |

| Attribute | Definition |
|---|---|
| | denomination, country of issue, country of registration, fees paid, letters of credit, etc. |
| Offering details | Details on the actual offering event, including period, provisions for over allotment, etc. |
| Principal | The amount of capital that the bond represents. This value can change over time where portions of the bond are redeemed (via events such as calls, partial, maturities, puts, etc.). Terms for early redemption are covered in the prospectus of the instrument, if appropriate. |
| Coupon history | Likely the single most common attribute is the rate of interest to be paid. Not only is current coupon rate important, so too is a historical record of any changes, as such events will affect the instrument's cash flow to holders and thereby its overall value (reflected in the price). |
| Maturity details | As important as the coupon rate and history is the maturity of the instrument, whereupon principal is usually repaid. Any change to the maturity – whether provided for in the terms of the instrument or otherwise – impacts on the time that the principal is in the hands of the issuer. A longer maturity than originally expected obviously impacts on the total value of the investment over the period. |
| Default information | Details related to default by the issuer and a related historical record. A history of defaults could suggest a riskier investment. |
| Collateral details | Collateral is pledged to secure the principal. As bond holders usually have first call on pledged assets, this information is very important to potential investors. |
| Bond features | Details associated with specific instruments. Common features include callable, retractable, extendible, etc. |
| Insurance details | Some bond terms include the purchase of insurance to ensure against failure of payment or principal repayment. Such provisions are intended to improve the rating applied to the security. |
| Third parties | All debt issues involve a relatively high degree of servicing which are typically outsourced to third-party service providers. Examples include transfer agents, registration agents, custodians, etc. |
| Benchmark details | Many bonds are issued on the basis of a difference from some other benchmark security such as a government bond. Details that are typically provided are instrument identifier of the benchmark, spread over benchmark yield, etc. |

## Redemption information

Instruments that provide a committed payment stream typically include the notion of redeeming the principal to the investor. This subtype provides the means of tracking how a particular instrument, such as a bond, is redeemed. There are two possibilities:

1.  The instrument (usually a bond) matures and the principal is repaid in full
2.  The terms of the instrument allow for redemptions to be conducted maturity to maturity, usually on a predetermined schedule.

| Attribute | Definition |
| --- | --- |
| Instrument identifier | An alphanumeric string used to identify securities. There are many different schemes in use to identify securities as well as international standards such as ISIN. As a result, cross-referencing between the various coding schemes is a fundamental requirement for working with market data. |
| Event identifier | A unique identifier value (usually a number) used to identify the event. Identifiers are important, as they allow for separate events affecting a given security to be recorded. |
| Redemption type | The manner in which the redemption is conducted – one of maturity, call or put in most cases. |
| Redemption date/schedule | The date range when the redemption takes place; can be a single date for maturities or a range for other event types. |
| Redemption details | Specific details associated with the redemption event. Usually includes specific items such as price, amount (for partial redemptions), notification periods, mandatory or optional, refunding provisions, etc. |

## Floating rate notes

Following the drill-down approach of the logical framework, this subtype captures the details that describe the terms under which a floating instrument resets its payment rate. This information is unique to a fixed income subclass called 'floating rate notes' (FRNs), or 'floaters' for short.

| Attribute | Definition |
|---|---|
| Instrument identifier | An alphanumeric string used to identify securities. There are many different schemes in use to identify securities as well as international standards such as ISIN. As a result, cross-referencing between the various coding schemes is a fundamental requirement for working with market data. |
| Event identifier | A unique identifier value (usually a number) used to identify the event. Identifiers are important, as they allow for separate events affecting a given security to be recorded. |
| FRN description | A textual description of the floating rate note. A variety of naming conventions are used for quick reference by market participants. |
| FRN type | Indicates the method by which a floating rate note's coupon is reset. |
| Coupon maximum | The highest rate at which a coupon rate may be reset for a particular formula. This rate is in effect throughout the formula effective period, as indicated by a change in the effective date. |
| Coupon minimum | The maximum decrease between the last coupon and the current coupon – that is, the maximum value that may be subtracted from the last coupon to set the current coupon. |
| Coupon rate reset formula | Usually provided by data sources as textual description, defines the process by which the new coupon rate is determined. Includes information on the benchmark, spreads, etc. |
| Reset schedule | The calendar dates on which the reset of the coupon are scheduled to take place. Depending on the data source, this can be a preset list of date values or a formula (e.g. first business day of each calendar quarter). |
| Reset history | A combination of the reset date, previous and reset coupon rate. Provides an audit trail to changes in the rate of cash flow generated by the security. |

(*Continued*)

| Attribute | Definition |
|---|---|
| Benchmark details | Identifying the benchmark; the index, or the specific security; off of which the coupon rate for a floating rate note is reset. This item, together with benchmark period and benchmark period term, provides a description of the benchmark. |
| Reset notification requirements | Captures any terms that require the issuer to notify holders of the reset event. Not frequently included, as the reset events are typically determined in advance by formula. |
| Effective date | The first date on which a reset methodology goes into effect. It should be used to identify which reset methodology is in effect, and the data associated with that methodology. |

## Sinking funds

This subtype captures information related to arrangements made by issuers to assemble funds over time to repay principal. Securities with such funds attached are typically viewed as lower risk to investors, as provisions for repayment of the principal are part of the terms.

| Attribute | Definition |
|---|---|
| Instrument identifier | An alphanumeric string used to identify securities. There are many different schemes in use to identify securities as well as international standards such as ISIN. As a result, cross-referencing between the various coding schemes is a fundamental requirement for working with market data. |
| Event identifier | A unique identifier value (usually a number) used to identify the event. Identifiers are important, as they allow for separate events affecting a given security to be recorded. |
| Sinking fund terms | A series of attributes that layout in detail the provisions of the bond related to any attached sinking fund. Typically include such items as the method used, bond anniversary date, requirements, timing, etc. |
| Sinking fund events | Records the enacting of the sinking fund terms. Attributes include mandatory indicator, amount, price, start date, end date. |

### Municipal bonds

Principally (but not exclusively) of interest to investors in the USA, this fixed income sub-type represents a very large and relatively liquid market, as associated income is tax free for qualified holders (qualification usually relates to state of residence for tax purposes). As such, there is a universe of attributes that provide specialist detail on these instruments, thereby allowing municipal bonds to be considered as a separate subtype. Indeed, within financial firms, municipal bond dealing is often handled by a dedicated desk.

| Attribute | Definition |
| --- | --- |
| Instrument identifier | An alphanumeric string used to identify securities. There are many different schemes in use to identify securities as well as international standards such as ISIN. As a result, cross-referencing between the various coding schemes is a fundamental requirement for working with market data. |
| Event identifier | A unique identifier value (usually a number) used to identify the event. Identifiers are important, as they allow for separate events affecting a given security to be recorded. |
| Municipal details | A wide variety of attributes and features that describe the instrument fully. Examples include insurance indicators (insurance guaranteeing payments to investors is often a requirement in order to achieve a good rating), bond type, the project being funded, the series of the bond, etc. |
| Tender details | Municipal bonds are considered to be highly secure investments, and as such the tender process, whereby new issues are brought to market, is closely followed. |
| Use of proceeds | Attributes that describe the manner in which the funds raised from the sale of the bonds will be used. |
| Third parties | Municipal bonds make extensive use of third-party service providers. |
| Underwriting details | Attributes that represent the activities associated with bringing the instrument to market and the related take-up by investors. As for any security, the underwriting process is extremely important in placing the issue with investors in a timely manner and thereby making the resulting funding available for use by the issuer. |

*(Continued)*

| Attribute | Definition |
|---|---|
| Credit details | In order to improve investment ratings, municipal bonds often include provisions such as insurance and guarantors to improve credit worthiness. This allows the bond to considered as a candidate for portfolios with ratings based investment criteria. |
| Tax rules | A series of attributes that identify the tax treatment for both qualified and non-qualified investors. Tax treatment is a major factor in decisions to purchase municipal bonds. |

## Structured products

Structured products is a highly specialized fixed income asset subtype within the logical framework. These instruments are structured (hence the name) around cash flows from other forms of borrowing as the collateral. Examples of structured products include:

- Collateralized mortgage obligations
- Mortgage backed securities
- Asset backed securities.

| Attribute | Definition |
|---|---|
| Instrument identifier | An alphanumeric string used to identify securities. There are many different schemes in use to identify securities as well as international standards such as ISIN. As a result, cross-referencing between the various coding schemes is a fundamental requirement for working with market data. |
| Event identifier | A unique identifier value (usually a number) used to identify the event. Identifiers are important, as they allow for separate events affecting a given security to be recorded. |
| Bond subtype details | The market accepted categorization of these securities. Usual designations are Mortgage Backed Security (MBS), Collateralized Mortgage Obligations (CMO), Collateralized Debt Obligations (CDO), and Asset Backed Securities (ABS). The designation is important, as it is associated with a particular segment of the market. From the data perspective, this manifests itself as different sets of attributes (and data quality) based on the type of instrument. |

| Attribute | Definition |
|---|---|
| Factors | Widely followed by investors and analysts, factors indicate the ratio of principal outstanding to the original principal balance associated with the collateral underlying the instruments (typically mortgages and other debt). Early repayment reduces the overall principal outstanding, thereby affecting the cash flow generated over the life of the security. |
| Collateral details | Specific information related to the collateral and how it is referred to by the security associated with the instrument identifier. Examples include details on pools, tranches, maturity dates, interest accrual, payment rates and schedules, etc. |
| Statistics | Statistical measures associated with structured products are used extensively by analysts. Associated attributes include the statistic type, the value and the date. Examples include duration, weighted average maturity, weighted average coupon, etc. |
| Prepayment information | Information related to the prepayment of principal on underlying collateral. Mortgage and other collateral typically are associated with fixed periods over which repayment is scheduled to occur. As such, prepayment results in the reduction of outstanding principal, thereby affecting the cash flow generated over the life of the security. |
| Payment information | Structured products instruments have a widely varying mix of interest and capital repayments as part of their terms. Understanding the mix that applies for a given instrument is therefore essential for calculating the rate of return over time to the investor. |
| Risk factors | Identification of the type of analysis, such as volatility, used to assess the fund's risk profile. A variety of factors is followed and used in order to asses the risk to which the investor is exposed. As with all statistical measures, both the date and reporting period are essential related attributes. |

## Data subtype: payment information

This subtype collects together attributes that describe the manner in which payments are made for income-producing instruments. As the income stream produced by an instrument over time is fundamental in valuing a security, this is critical information in determining the projected rate of return.

| Attribute | Definition |
|-----------|------------|
| Instrument identifier | An alphanumeric string used to identify securities. There are many different schemes in use to identify securities as well as international standards such as ISIN. As a result, cross-referencing between the various coding schemes is a fundamental requirement for working with market data. |
| Payment terms | A collection of attributes that detail the income stream to be provided by the security. Typical payment terms include the frequency, method, record date, pay pate, ex-date, settlement date, etc. |
| Payment events | Attributes that describe individual payments made. Typically does not include regularly scheduled payments such as coupon interest. Attributes include the schedule and history of the payment, the amount, the currency (or in kind payment in some cases), the record date, etc. |
| Event identifier | A unique identifier value (usually a number) used to identify the event. Identifiers are important, as they allow for separate events affecting a given security to be recorded. |
| Payment details | Associated with any specific payment are a number of specific details that describe the specific payment. Payment details should be considered as optional attributes as regularly scheduled and fulfilled payments that meet the terms of the instrument's prospectus, require little explanatory detail. |
| Accrual information | Details the rules by which missed income payments, if any, are accumulated and repaid. Attributes include the amount, the start and end dates for the period over which the accrual takes place, and the type of accrual (usually associated with detailed terms of the instrument). |

### Data subtype: collective investments

This subtype groups together attributes associated with instruments that are made up of other instruments (commonly referred to as funds). A very diverse universe of instruments, common attributes include the following.

| Attribute | Definition |
|---|---|
| Instrument identifier | An alphanumeric string used to identify securities. There are many different schemes in use to identify securities as well as international standards such as ISIN. As a result, cross-referencing between the various coding schemes is a fundamental requirement for working with market data. |
| Fund name | A textual description of the fund. |
| Management firm | The name of the firm (potentially an issuer entity itself) that is responsible for the management of the holdings of the fund. |
| Fund type | Attributes that describe the general type of collective investment. Examples include open or closed end fund, passive or active, socially responsible fund, etc. |
| Fees | All fund managers charge a variety of fees to their investors. Examples include management fees, administration fees, distribution costs, etc. |
| Investor details | Other information not covered in the general security descriptive information. Typical examples include minimum investment size, unit value at day of purchase, processing time requirements, minimum holding period, load type, etc. |

## Holdings

This provides details regarding the constituents making up the portfolio of the fund.

| Attribute | Definition |
|---|---|
| Instrument identifier | An alphanumeric string used to identify securities. There are many different schemes in use to identify securities as well as international standards such as ISIN. As a result, cross-referencing between the various coding schemes is a fundamental requirement for working with market data. |
| Constituents | The individual instruments making up the collective investment (typically an investment fund). These instruments can be recorded as part of the relations data subtype, but are often delivered as part of the textual description of the fund. Note that constituents change over time, and therefore are usually coupled with revision dates. |

*(Continued)*

| Attribute | Definition |
| --- | --- |
| Asset breakdown | The holdings of the fund broken down by asset type. Many investment funds seek to maximize rate of return with minimum risk by diversifying across asset types. Evaluating the fund based on the percentage allocated to different asset classes is a common criteria applied by investors and analysts. |
| Asset details | Additional details specific to the individual constituents making up the fund. Most of this information duplicates other information that is defined within this framework, and tends to be delivered as part of the textual description provided by data vendors and the fund's management. |
| Geographic breakdown | The percentage allocation of assets making up the fund, based on country, region or other geographic criteria. Assessing the fund on these terms is relatively common, as it incorporates the risk to which the fund is exposed globally. This incorporates a variety of factors, such as currency and political risk – among others. |
| Rating breakdown | A summary of the allocation of assets classified by the investment rating of the constituent securities. This criterion provides investors with a measure of the perceived risk associated with the portfolio of the fund. |

## Management

This captures the set of attributes that relate to how the fund is managed.

| Attribute | Definition |
| --- | --- |
| Instrument identifier | An alphanumeric string used to identify securities. There are many different schemes in use to identify securities as well as international standards such as ISIN. As a result, cross-referencing between the various coding schemes is a fundamental requirement for working with market data. |
| Style | Definition of the style of investment and strategy that the management follows. An important criterion for investors. |
| Investment criteria | An indication of the criteria applied by the management to determine whether a security meets the fund's investment strategy and objectives. |

| Attribute | Definition |
| --- | --- |
| Personnel | Details on financial professionals who are assigned to manage and/or administer the individual fund identified by the instrument identifier. Details include names, education and certifications, start date, tenure, other investments managed. |

## Performance

A series of attributes that capture the measures of the fund's performance over time. A wide variety of statistical values are used in the industry, including both absolute and relative measures.

| Attribute | Definition |
| --- | --- |
| Instrument identifier | An alphanumeric string used to identify securities. There are many different schemes in use to identify securities as well as international standards such as ISIN. As a result, cross-referencing between the various coding schemes is a fundamental requirement for working with market data. |
| Annual reports | An annual report to investors is required of all funds. |
| Reporting date(s) | As with any measurement of performance, the date on which the report is made is fundamental to assessing the results. |
| Reporting period | Identification of the calendar period for which the report is made. |
| Yields | The rate of return achieved by the investment over the reporting period. |
| Returns | Measures of the various forms of return to the investor. Examples include return, total return (e.g. including dividend or coupon reinvestment, etc.), risk-adjusted return, etc. |
| Statistics | A wide variety of statistical measures are used by the industry as a means of measuring performance. To be relevant, statistics need to refer to both the reporting date and period. |
| Performance ratings | Many funds are tracked by third-party analysts and other firms. The fund's performance is evaluated against their peers and the financial industry in general. A variety of rating schemes are used, depending on the agency. |

**Risk measures**

A fundamental criterion of fundamental importance to all investors is the risk associated with purchasing financial instruments. Risk measures for collective investments are widely available and cover an extensive range.

| Attribute | Definition |
|---|---|
| Instrument identifier | An alphanumeric string used to identify securities. There are many different schemes in use to identify securities as well as international standards such as ISIN. As a result, cross-referencing between the various coding schemes is a fundamental requirement for working with market data. |
| Metric type | Identification of the type of analysis, such as volatility, used to assess the fund's risk profile. |
| Metric value | The actual value associated with the metric type. |
| Period | Identification of the calendar period for which the metric applies. |
| Date | The calendar date on which the metric is produced. |
| Commentary | Additional textual commentary is commonly provided with assessment of risk measures. Identification of the analyst is also quite frequently included, reflecting the influence of the analyst on the sector. |

## Data subtype: *clearing information*

The act of clearing is fundamental to the global capital markets. Transactions between counterparties need to be matched and confirmed before securities and cash can change hands. This subtype lays out the universe of attributes that are typically encountered and relate to this activity.

| Attribute | Definition |
|---|---|
| Instrument identifier | An alphanumeric string used to identify securities. There are many different schemes in use to identify securities as well as international standards such as ISIN. As a result, cross-referencing between the various coding schemes is a fundamental requirement for working with market data. |

| Attribute | Definition |
|---|---|
| Country/countries | Geographic identification of the clearing location is critical, as different countries have different rules and conventions. |
| Clearing type | The method of clearing that is used. Typically handled by third-party agencies. |
| Clearing agency/ agencies | Identification of the clearing agency used to match the orders making up a transaction between counterparties. |
| Clearing schedule | The timeframe on which the transaction must be matched and confirmed. Most markets have predetermined conventions depending on asset type. |
| Third-party information | Identification of other third-party service providers associated with the clearing process. |
| Eligibility | A coded value that identifies the eligibility of the security for clearing purposes. Not all securities are necessarily supported by any one agency, so, as a result, identification of this attribute can be very important to the counterparties involved in a transaction. |
| Clearing details | A series of attributes that define the rules and procedures associated with the clearing agency. Typically includes concepts such as filing dates, levels of service for confirmation, etc. |

## Data subtype: tax information

Taxation impacts on the net rate of return of an investment, and therefore is of fundamental importance to holders of securities. Data of this nature is typically quite complex and very specific to individual tax regimes. Tax information is further complicated by different rules for different asset classes, and is therefore considered within asset-specific business data.

| Attribute | Definition |
|---|---|
| Instrument identifier | An alphanumeric string used to identify securities. There are many different schemes in use to identify securities as well as international standards such as ISIN. As a result, cross-referencing between the various coding schemes is a fundamental requirement for working with market data. |

*(Continued)*

| Attribute | Definition |
|---|---|
| Geographic identifiers | A fundamental attribute associated with taxation is the country and/or other regulatory regime (e.g. state, province) to which the tax applies. Tax rates and other rules differ markedly based on geographic criteria, as does the issue of residency within the location. |
| Taxable indicator | A coded value that indicates whether or not gains on the investment are subject to tax. |
| Tax type | Usually a coded value with an associated textual definition that identifies the specific tax to which the security is exposed. Tax types vary widely depending on geography and regulatory framework, and are known to change over time. |
| Tax details | Usually provided as textual information, provides definitions related to the tax rule that applies to the instrument. |
| Tax thresholds and triggers | Commonly encountered in information services are the trigger points at which gains from investments become taxable. These attributes provide the basis upon which it is possible to determine whether the investment requires a tax payment, and can therefore be referred to as 'determination events'. |
| Payment rules | Attributes that define how any payments (or possibly refunds) are to be submitted to the taxing authority, and related schedule requirements. |
| Reporting requirements | A series of attributes that define the manner in which gains from an investment (whether income of capital gains) are to be reported to the taxing authority. Some sources provide details on specific forms to be completed, and filing requirements. |

# Index